EXPLORING THE VALUE AND SIGNIFICANCE OF GHANA IN TODAY'S GLOBAL LANDSCAPE

Does the World Need Ghana?

Yemi Adesina

Disclaimer

Every reasonable effort was made to ensure that the material in this book is accurate, correct, complete and appropriate in writing. Nevertheless, the publishers and the author do not accept responsibility for any omission or error or any injury, damage, loss or financial consequences arising from the use of this book. Views expressed in the articles are those of the author and not the Editor or Publisher.

ISBN: 979-8-39871-806-5

CONTENTS

Apologia

There are bound to be — only a few, I hope — errors and omissions, and I apologise in advance. No man knows it all, especially me! And you learn more as you get older. One good thing that comes with age is that you are happy to confess when you don't know and pass the inquiry on to a specialist who probably does.

This book is dedicated to hardworking, patient, enthusiastic, generally under-rewarded, and underappreciated people of Africa, those at home and in the diaspora and everyone interested in the welfare of the continent of Africa.

Kwame Nkrumah's Quotes

"The independence of Ghana is meaningless unless it is linked up with the total liberation of the African continent."

"I am not African because I was born in Africa, but because Africa was born in me."

"All people of African descent, whether they live in North or South America, the Caribbean, or any part of the world, are Africans and belong to the African nation."

Foreword

Ghana has a long and rich history, from its ancient empires to its colonial past to its present-day role as a leader in West Africa and beyond. As an expert in African history and development, I have spent decades visiting and studying the country and its people and have come to appreciate the depth of Ghana's cultural, political, and economic contributions to the African continent and the world.

Situated in West Africa, Ghana was the first African country to gain independence from colonial rule in 1957 under the leadership of Kwame Nkrumah. Since then, Ghana has played a significant role in the global community, both politically and culturally.

In this book, we examine whether the world needs Ghana. We explore Ghana's contributions to the world and examine the country's potential to continue to make a positive impact in the future. We also consider Ghana's challenges in its development efforts and the role the international community can play in supporting these efforts.

As Ghana faces various challenges, including poverty, inequality, corruption, and environmental degradation, it is important to understand its strengths and weaknesses and appreciate its unique contributions to the global community. By shedding light on Ghana's complex history and contemporary realities, this book seeks to inform policymakers, scholars, and the general public about the country's potential and ongoing struggles and contribute to a more nuanced and accurate understanding of Ghana's place in the world.

This book draws on my expertise as an African historian and my development experience gained through my work in Africa. It provides a comprehensive analysis of Ghana's past and present and offers insights into the future of this important country.

The book is organised into several chapters, each exploring different aspects of Ghana's history, culture, economy, and politics. Chapters one to three provides an overview of Ghana's historical and cultural significance, tracing its roots back to its ancient empires and exploring the impact of colonialism and post-colonialism on Ghana's development.

Chapters four and five examine Ghana's location, cultural contributions to the world, including its role in the fight for African independence, its leadership in Pan-Africanism and the Non-Aligned Movement, and its contributions to the arts, music, and literature.

Chapter Six explores Ghana's natural resources, including gold, Cocoa, and oil, and their impact on the global economy. It examines Ghana's challenges in its development efforts, including the impact of colonialism, corruption, and political instability, and its efforts to overcome them. It also looks at Ghana's role in the global context, including its participation in regional and global economic and political organisations, its contributions to the Sustainable Development Goals (SDGs), and its partnerships and collaborations with other countries and organisations.

The book considers the future of Ghana, including its potential to become a leading player in the global economy, its efforts to build a sustainable future, and the challenges that must be overcome to achieve its development goals. Finally, Chapter Eight summarises the book's key arguments and findings and emphasises the importance of supporting Ghana's development efforts.

Overall, this book provides a comprehensive and insightful assessment of Ghana's place globally, highlighting the country's strengths, weaknesses, and unique contributions to global society. We hope to shed light on the significant contributions that this country has made to the world and the challenges and opportunities that lie ahead.

Acknowledgements

Although one man has written this book, it wouldn't have been possible without the many people who have been so inspirational and whose research and hard work were helpful during its writing.

I thank God Almighty for His grace to research and put my findings into a book.

I also owe much to the many people who have encouraged me to follow my dream. In particular, my late dad, Mr Solomon Olajide Adesina. And to Bola, my wife of 27 years of marriage. I thank her immensely for her undying love, support, and encouragement, which allowed me to travel, research, and practise farming in Africa for many years.

For my two sons, Femi and Seun, whose input as the second-generation African diaspora in the United Kingdom makes the book more relevant to younger Africans. I want to thank them for our lengthy chats and the healthy debates that lasted late into the night and early mornings to gather their perspectives on specific topics. I firmly believe their generation and those following beyond will move Africa further into the future.

Many people influenced me to start learning about Africa. Some of them I have met in person, and some I know through their teachings, lectures, training, research books and journals. Coming from all walks of life, the variety of sources, expertise and professions assisted me in approaching the issue from different perspectives, adding much value to this book.

My inspirations were Pastor Matthew Ashimolowo, the late Dr Myles Munro, Dr Mensah Otabil, and Bishop Tudor Bismark. These pastors spent a lot of time teaching and believing Africa could improve.

I am greatly indebted to Dr Toyin Falola, an African historian, Dr Howard Nicholas, an economist and researcher at Erasmus University Rotterdam, and Jeffrey D. Sachs et al. for their input on the impact of geography. I am further indebted to Quoras.com, Walter Rodney *for How Europe Underdeveloped Africa.* Finally, I thank Yemi Adeyemi, the founder of ThinkAfrica.net.

The Author

Mr Yemi Adesina is the founder of Boyd Agro-Allied Ltd, one of the largest pig farms in Nigeria. He is also the CEO of Pristine Integrated Farm Resources Ltd, a non-profit organisation registered in Africa to promote youth and rural empowerment, alleviate poverty in Africa through education, and improve the productivity and livelihood of farmers from subsistence to commercial farming in Africa.

He is a qualified social worker, a seasoned farmer and a prolific trainer. He posted 150 videos on YouTube (papayemo1) covering pig farming and African History. Over 2.5 million viewers watched the videos in over 36 countries, making it one of the most-watched videos on YouTube from an African perspective.

He is the author of "*Why Africa Cannot Feed Itself and the Way Forward*", "*Profitable Pig Farming: A Step-by-Step Guide to Commercial Pig Farming from an African Perspective*", "*What the Ancient African Knew*", "*Does the World Need Africa*", *Nigeria: A Complex Nation at a Crossroads in Africa and the World*, and "The Unsettled Debt: Examining the Responsibility of the World towards the Democratic Republic of Congo".

Mr Yemi, a diaspora, emigrated to the United Kingdom in 1991. He studied and worked for 20 years and earned his Master's in Business Administration and Master's in Social Work in the United Kingdom. In 2010, he emigrated to Nigeria to contribute to Nigeria's food production.

1. Introduction

Geography studies the Earth's physical features, land, water, atmosphere, and relationship with man's activities. Ancient Precambrian cratons (an ancient part of the Earth's continental crust) formed the land of the African continent a long time ago, between about 3.6 and 2 billion years ago, making the tectonic table of the continent very stable. The land rarely moves, so there are hardly any earthquakes or volcanoes. All of the rocks on the continent have been extensively folded and metamorphosed by heat and pressure over time.

As elsewhere in Africa, the climate of Ghana 12,000 years ago was characterised by heavy rainfall as the forest spread northward and humans retreated toward the Sahara. Between 9000 and 4000 BC, the Sahara had a dry subtropical climate characterised by a freezing winter, a scorching summer, annual high-temperature ranges, and rain. The rain usually fell in August, causing flash floods transporting water to the other parts of the desert.

During this period, the Sahara was more humid, held numerous lakes, had rife vegetation, and covered tropical savanna grasslands teemed with wild animals, all encouraging human settlement. However, in 2,000 BC, the rainfall pattern in the Sahara changed and gradually decreased to form a much drier and hotter climate. This change turned the grasslands of the Sahara into a desert permanently.

With increased aridity, humans moved back along the Togo mountain range from the Niger River towards modern-day Ghana. Sangoan tools abound in Transvolta and around Accra and extend to Kumasi; the West remained forest. The Sangoan and Lupemban cultures emerged from the desiccating Sahara; they occurred in valleys' basal gravels. Their shapely, crude, formless tools are found in central Ghana near the coast.

Ghana's historical significance can be traced back to its ancient empires, which were among Africa's most advanced and sophisticated. Ghana's ancient empires and kingdoms profoundly impacted the development of other West African empires, such as the Mali Empire, the Songhai Empire, and the Kanem-Bornu Empire. These empires also significantly impacted the development of the trans-Saharan trade routes, which connected West Africa to North Africa and the Middle East.

1.1. THE GHANA EMPIRE

Although the rest of sub-Saharan Africa did not begin adopting agriculture until 1000 BCE or later, West Africa started to launch into developed agricultural civilisations around 3000 BCE, like the Fertile Crescent in EuroAsia. This development led to a "food bonanza" that supported many more people in a settled community than a hunter-gathering lifestyle in a given land area.

The agricultural civilisation led to the emergence of complex societies in West Africa around 1500 BCE, and the region's archaeology reveals several settlements. By 600 BCE, there were some large towns and villages in West Africa where there was enough of an agricultural surplus that not everybody needed to farm but could perform the duties of rulers, artisans, engineers, and bureaucrats. During this period, many African cultures used iron technology, such as hoe and cutlasses, further increasing farming productivity.

While many city-states and small kingdoms existed in West Africa for centuries, the Ghana Empire was the first major agricultural Empire to arise in the region. Its history is shrouded in mystery. The tradition of the Ghana empire refers to a founder called Dingha Kaya Magar Cissé, a man "from the east". A king of a realm called Wagadou rose to prominence in West Africa around 300 CE. The name Ghana means "warrior king" in Soninke, a language from the region of the Empire of Ghana. The sons and grandsons of this king further extended their rule over several other kingdoms, turning the Ghana empire into a vassal state. Many of the names of the Ghana rulers are unknown, and only a few of their deeds have passed into recorded history.

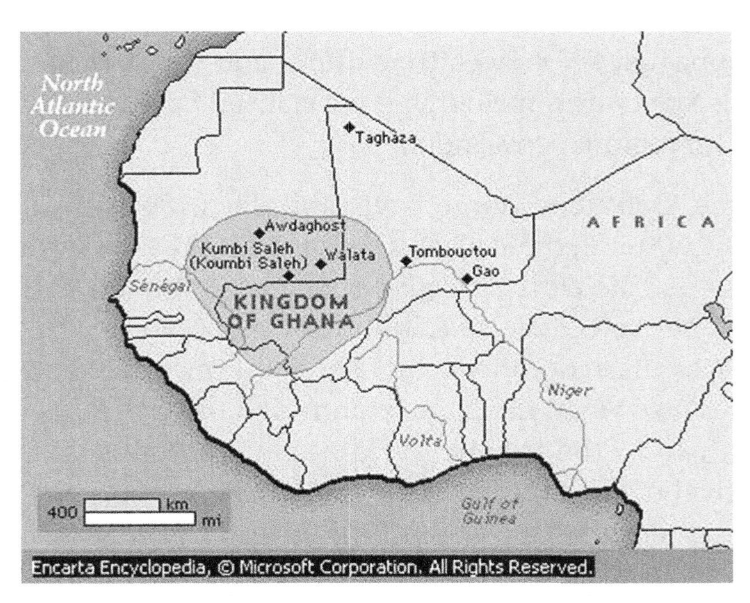

A map of Ancient GhanaEmpire. Source: Encarta Encyclopedia

Archeologist believes that, around 300 CE, West Africans domesticated the camel as an efficient form of transport across the desert. Camels revolutionised trade across the Sahara. Rapidly growing trade brought a lot of wealth and power to West Africa, just as the Ghana Empire was getting its start. The kingdom covered 250,000 square kilometres and over a population of 3 million.

The Ghana Empire, in particular, grew rich from the trans-Sahara trade. The trans-Sahara trade helped the Empire to have control over the three major gold fields. Traders referred to Ghana as "the Land of Gold," and the kings of Ghana were sometimes called "the Lords of the Gold." As a result, the Empire flourished. The king of Ghana monopolised all gold nuggets found in the mines; the people were allowed to trade in gold dust but had to turn over any gold nuggets to the government. As such, the state also became very powerful, adding to the complexity of Ghana's agricultural civilisation. The Empire was renowned for its wealth, culture, and sophisticated governance structures, including a centralised bureaucracy and a system of regional governors.

Once the Arabs moved into Egypt and Northwest Africa in the 600s and 700s CE, trade intensified, and Ghana grew even more prosperous. The West Africans became major traders in the Old World. They sold ivory, salt, iron tools and weapons, furniture, textiles, sandals, herbs, spices, fish, rice, honey, and kola nuts. This was also when the large exportation of slave labour from West Africa to the Islamic world began. Centuries later, with the arrival of the Portuguese, a similar exportation of African people as slave labour would further lead to the massive coerced exodus of Africans to the Americas. It was the monopoly on West African gold, however, that allowed the Ghana Empire to reach the height of its power at a time when Europe was undergoing a decline after the fall of the Roman Empire. Ghana's rule extended as far as the Niger Valley.

Many historians wondered how such a massive empire was built in the Sahel region, where the climate was dry, and drinking water was scarce. Historians believe that, unlike Egypt, which depended on the Nile River, the Ghana empire constructed many wells to support its populace and irrigate plants grown within the city. The fact that 15,000 to 20,000 people were able to live in a city so close to the harsh Sahara desert is an astounding feat of architecture and engineering.

The Old Ghana Empire. Source: gajreport.com

Historians believe the Ghana empire traded its gold by 'silent' or 'mute' barter. Barter is a method by which traders who cannot speak each other's language can trade without talking. Group A would leave trade goods in a prominent position and beat great drums to inform the locals that they had left goods. Group B would then arrive at the spot, examine the goods, place a heap of gold beside each pile, and withdraw. Group A would then return and either accept the trade by taking the gold from Group B or withdraw again, leaving Group B to add or change items to create an equal value. The transaction ended when Group A accepted Group B's offer and removed the offered goods leaving Group B to remove the gold and retreat, beating their drums to signify that the market was over.

In the twelfth Century, Ghana began incorporating more Muslims into its government, including the Master of the treasury, diplomats, and most officials. By the end of the 1100s, Ghana had converted entirely to Islam. By 1200, however, Ghana became culturally incorporated into the Afro-Eurasian world zone as trade continued to share collective learning. West Africa sat at the very end of an extended network forming the Silk Roads that stretched across the Afro-Eurasian supercontinent.

Ghana's long period as the dominant agricultural civilisation of West Africa ended in the 1200s. The wet climate that had once made farming prosperous in the Sahel continued to deteriorate. With a dwindling water supply, resources and power, along with some political infighting, Ghana left a power vacuum that was soon filled. Rivals called the Sosso briefly occupied territories of Ghana, including its capital, and built their short-lived Empire. They, in turn, were conquered by the Mali Empire, which forged an even larger and wealthier empire in West Africa. They, in turn, were overthrown by the Songhai Empire in the 1400s. In the 1590s, however, the Songhai Empire fell mercilessly to the Moroccans.

With the death of Askia Muhammad, the Emperor of Songhai, in 1528 CE, the Songhai Empire started falling apart. Ahmad al-Mansur, the Emperor of Morocco, saw this as an opportunity to conquer the Empire after his Spanish humiliation. In 1591 CE, he sent an army of four thousand musketeers under the leadership of a Spanish mercenary officer called Judar Pasha. Despite the brave stand of the Songhai army, the Moroccan soldiers overwhelmed them with sophisticated military weapons and moved into the country to wreak havoc.

Prof. Clarke said, *"The Moroccan invasion of Songhai and other nations of Western Sudan was controversial and tragic because the war was Muslim against Muslim. The invaders from North Africa, Muslim Arabs and their European mercenary troops, did not spare anyone, not man, woman or child. They pitilessly slew everyone, even when women and children cried to the soldiers, we are your brothers in religion, and we are Muslims. The soldier slaughtered most of the black African Muslims while they were reciting their Shahada* .لا إله إلا الله (الله – لا يوجد شيء يستحق العبادة إلا الله) ومحمد رسول الله ".له واحد ورسوله"
This means, *"There is no God but God (Allah — i. e. there is none worthy of worship but Allah), and Muhammad is the Messenger of Allah."*

The war destroyed African intellectuals as leading scholars were chained and sent to Marrakesh. The wealth of Timbuktu, Gao, and Jenne was stripped, and vast quantities of gold dust, valued by an English merchant at £600,000, were shipped across the desert on thirty camels.

This chaos and devastation set up Africa for the intense European slave trade that followed. This trade in enslaved Africans, begun by the Arabs, went on uninterrupted from the 6th Century CE to the 15th Century CE and softened Africa militarily, culturally, economically, socially and politically. Arabs were also the principal raiders, merchants, and middlemen for the Atlantic slave trade.

The coordination of the black slave trade was more accessible for the Arabs because, in all areas conquered by Arabs in Africa, the natives lost their ethnic names, religions, and peculiar way of life to their Arab masters. The slaves colonised by Arabs were left bare, without a past or future. The Islamic religion and Arab culture overwhelmed African cultures and traditions wherever they conquered. Today, Africans in Arab-governed states no longer bear their original African names or remember their history. They cannot recall being Black, independent, and thriving communities before the Arabs colonised them.

1.2. THE GOLD COAST

The establishment of direct sea trade with Europe started when the Portuguese controlled the Atlantic coast of Morocco and used its economic and strategic advantages to further navigate from the West to the south of Africa, the Cape of Good Hope, in 1495. On the way back, the Portuguese mariners arrived on the coast of Ghana. Initially, Europe's main interest in the country was as a source of gold, a commodity readily available on the coast in exchange for such European exports as cloth, hardware, beads, metals, spirits, arms, and ammunition. This transaction gave rise to the name Gold Coast, by which the country was known until 1957. To preserve a trade monopoly, the Portuguese initiated erecting stone fortresses, like (Elmina Castle, dating from 1482, the oldest European building in sub-Saharan Africa. The presence of these permanent European bases on the coast had far-reaching consequences.

Elmina_Castle. Source: www.tripadvisor.com

The Portuguese started kidnapping people from the west coast of Africa and took them as a slave to Portugal. By the middle of the 16th Century, more than 10% of Lisbon's population was of African descent. In the 17th Century, the Portuguese monopoly gave way completely when traders from the Netherlands, England, Denmark, Sweden, and Prussia discovered the commercial potential of having a fort in the Gold Coast state to export slaves to America. By the mid-18th Century, the coastal scene was dominated by about 40 forts controlled by Dutch, British, or Danish merchants.

1.3. THE BEGINNING AND THE IMPACT OF SLAVERY IN GHANA

The act of slavery is as old as humanity itself. The concept of slavery has been around throughout the European Middle Ages, with the Crusades between Christians and Muslims giving an added excuse for enslaving people. The cultural set-up of the people of the West African coasts was no different at that time — it accepted slavery. Ghana was no exception; the traditional slave trade had been part and parcel of Africa before the arrival of Europeans. Obtaining captives on African soil was done through inter-tribal and communal warfare. That is, kings fought their neighbours and subdued prisoners. Typically, in ancient Africa, when someone was captured at war, he served as a slave for a short time. Captives or their offspring were then absorbed as ordinary members of society, especially if they had a skill or could prove valuable. There was no scope for the continual abuse of man by man in Africa during this period. The Arabs were the first to introduce the perpetual exploitation of slaves during the Trans-Sahara slave trade in East Africa and Sudan when Arabs took many Africans to Arab countries and Asia.

The introduction of European and American ships in the 17th Century and the offering of trading goods in exchange for people increased the demand for slaves. The demand dissolved the continent's ethical slave conventions that had governed slavery for centuries, leading to the 'degradation of slavery' and an added incentive for Africa to enslave each other.

Transatlantic slavery could never have happened without African collaboration. Some rulers or wealthy and influential African merchants motivated by their selfish interests joined to make slavery possible for the Europeans. They facilitated the movement of slaves from the inland to the port, and the Europeans loaded and shipped the slaves to America. Initially, these rulers found European goods sufficiently desirable to hand over captives they had taken from warfare. However, by the mid-17th Century, the European demand for more captives, particularly for the sugar plantations in the Americas, became so great that sufficient slaves could only be acquired through kidnapping, raiding, and warfare. Some societies preyed on others to obtain captives in exchange for European firearms. If they did not acquire firearms in this way to protect themselves, they would be attacked and captured by their rivals and enemies who did possess such weapons. Europeans took advantage of this situation and started playing African leaders, equipping them to challenge each other to obtain more slaves. Ultimately, Europe benefited from whichever of the two nations won the conflict.

The trans-Atlantic slave trade was fueled by European demand for labour in the Americas, and Ghana was a major source of slaves. European slave traders established trading posts along the Ghanaian coast, which became centres of the slave trade. They traded goods, such as textiles and guns, for slaves captured by African intermediaries who raided villages and kingdoms in the interior.

The impact of the trans-Atlantic slave trade on Ghana was devastating. It led to the depopulation of many areas, as people were captured and sold into slavery. It also disrupted many communities' social and economic systems, as people were torn away from their families and traditional livelihoods. The slave trade also created conflict between different ethnic groups, as some groups became involved in capturing and selling slaves, while slave raiders targeted others.

Slave Inspection. Source: *africanslavery1780s-blog.tumblr.co*

The new wealth, tools and arms, and techniques and ideas introduced through close contact with Europeans initiated political, social, and economic changes. By the end of the 17th Century, the Akan state of Akwamu created an empire stretching from the central Gold Coast eastward to Dahomey, seeking to control the trade roads to the coast of the whole eastern Gold Coast. The union of the Asante (Ashanti) states of the central forest, under the leadership of the founding Asantehene (king) Osei Tutu, established its dominance over other neighbouring Akan states. The Asante Union expanded north of the forest to conquer Bono, Banda, Gonja, and Dagomba. The Asante took over the market, the major supply for the coastal trade, and then turned toward the coastlands. In the late 18th Century, Asante armies invaded the coastal states, especially those that became European allies.

The legacy of slavery is still felt in Ghana today. Many Ghanaians are descendants of people captured and sold into slavery, and the trauma of that experience has been passed down through generations. Economic and social inequalities can be traced back to the slave trade, as some communities were more affected than others.

In recent years, there have been efforts to confront the legacy of slavery in Ghana. The government has established a national memorial to honour victims of the slave trade, and there have been calls for reparations for descendants of slaves. There have also been efforts to promote economic development in areas most affected by the slave trade to address some ongoing inequalities.

However, Ghana also played a role in resisting the slave trade. In the next section, we will see how some Ghanaian kingdoms, such as the Ashanti and Fante, resisted European encroachment on their territory and fought against the slave trade.

Queen Nanny

One such hero is Queen Nanny. Queen Nanny was born in Ghana in western Africa to the Ashanti tribe. Nanny and her four brothers were sold into slavery and later escaped from their plantations into the mountains and jungles of Jamaica.

Maroons were slaves in the Americas who escaped and formed independent settlements. Nanny eventually founded a village in the Blue Mountains, on the Eastern side of Jamaica, known as Nanny Town.

By 1720, Nanny had become the leader of this maroon settlement, where she trained her maroon warriors in the art of guerilla warfare due to incessant tension between her people and the British. According to history, Nanny Town thrived due to its location in the mountains away from European settlements. Nanny became the spiritual and military leader of the people of Nanny Town.

During a period of 30 years, she contributed to the escape of more than 1,000 slaves and helped them resettle in the Maroon community.

1.4. ANGLO-ASHANTI WARS

The Asante Empire was an Akan state that lasted from 1701 to 1901 in modern-day Ghana. It expanded from the Ashanti Region to include most of Ghana and parts of Ivory Coast and Togo. Due to the Empire's military prowess, wealth, architecture, sophisticated hierarchy and culture, the Ashanti Empire has been extensively studied. It has more historical records written by European, primarily British, authors than any other indigenous culture of Sub-Saharan Africa.

The Anglo-Ashanti wars were a series of five conflicts that took place between 1824 and 1900 between the Ashanti Empire and the British Empire and its African allies. The wars were mainly due to Ashanti's attempts to maintain and enforce their imperial stronghold over the coastal areas of present-day Ghana, where peoples such as the Fante and Ga had come under the protection of the British. Although the Ashanti emerged victorious in some of these conflicts, the British ultimately prevailed in the fourth and fifth conflicts, resulting in the complete annexation of the Ashanti Empire by 1900.

The British fought some preliminary wars with Ashanti on the Gold Coast:

During the Ashanti-Fante War of 1806–07, the British refused to hand over two rebels pursued by the Ashanti. In the Ga-Fante War of 1811, the Ashanti sought to aid their Ga allies in a war against the Fante and their British allies. The Ashanti army won the initial battles and captured a British fort at Tantamkweri.

In the Ashanti-Akim-Akwapim War of 1814–16, the Ashanti defeated the Akim-Akwapim alliance. Local British, Dutch, Polish, and Danish authorities had to come to terms with the Ashanti. By 1817, the Ashanti had an army of about 200,000, so the British signed a treaty of friendship that recognised Ashanti's claims to sovereignty over much of the coast.

First Anglo-Ashanti War, 1823–1831

By the 1820s, the British had decided to support the Fante against Ashanti raids from the inland. Ashanti kidnapped and murdered an African service member and led a group of British soldiers into a trap, resulting in 10 killed, 39 wounded, and a British retreat. MacCarthy led an invading force from the Cape

Coast, where the British were confronted by a force of 10,000 well-disciplined Ashanti men armed with their "Long Dane" muskets. The Ashanti generally did not have bullets, so they used nails instead, which proved an effective substitute. The British ran out of ammunition, almost all British forces were killed, and only 20 managed to escape.

The new Governor of the Gold Coast, John Hope Smith, started to gather 11,000 new soldiers, mainly comprised of natives, many of the traditional enemies of the Ashanti. In August 1826, the Governor heard that the Ashanti were planning on attacking Accra. On August 7, the Ashanti army attacked the centre of the British line where the best troops were held, including some Royal Marines, the militia and a battery of Congreve rockets. The novelty of the weapons, the explosions, rocket trails, and grievous wounds caused by flying metal shards caused the Ashanti to fall back. In 1831, a treaty accepted the Pra River as the border.

Second Anglo-Ashanti War

The second Anglo-Ashanti War took place between 1863 and 1864. In 1863, a large Ashanti force crossed the Pra River in search of a fugitive, Kwesi Gyana. British, African and Indian troops responded, but neither side claimed victory as illness took more casualties than the actual fighting. The Second War ended in 1864, and the result was a stalemate.

Third Anglo-Ashanti War 1873–1874

The Third Anglo-Ashanti War, also known as the "First Ashanti Expedition", lasted from 1873 to 1875. The British Gold Coast was formally established in 1867, and in 1872, Britain expanded its territory when it purchased the Dutch Gold Coast from the Dutch, including Elmina, which the Ashanti claimed. The

Dutch signed the Treaty of Butre in 1656 with the Ashanti. This all changed with the sale of the Dutch Gold Coast, and the Ashanti invaded the new British protectorate.

Ashanti warriors. Source *www.menofthewest.net/*

General Garnet Wolseley was sent against the Ashanti with 2,500 British and several thousand West Indian and African troops.

In total, 237 Bridges were built across streams using trees, bamboo and creepers for ropes, and a major bridge across the 63 yards (58 m)-wide River Prah was built using pre-manufactured pieces brought from Chatham, England.

The Battle of Amoaful was fought on January 31. A road was cut to the village and with the pipes playing "The Campbells Are Coming", the Black Watch charged with bayonets, and the shocked Ashantis fled.

The Ashanti abandoned the capital, Kumasi, when the British arrived on February 4. The British demolished the royal palace with explosives, leaving Kumasi a heap of smouldering ruins. The British were impressed by the size of the palace and the scope of its contents, including "rows of books in many languages. The Ashanti later signed the Treaty of Fomena in July 1874 to end the war. The King of Ashanti promises to pay the sum of 50,000 ounces of approved gold as indemnity for the expenses he has occasioned to Her Majesty the Queen of England by the late war..."

Burning of Kumasi depicted by Henry Morton Stanley.
Source: *https://en.wikipedia.org/*

Some British accounts pay tribute to the hard fighting of the Ashanti at Amoaful, particularly the tactical insight of their commander, Amankwatia."

Fourth Anglo-Ashanti War

The Fourth Anglo-Ashanti War, also known as the "Second Ashanti Expedition", was brief, lasting only from December 26 1895 to February 4 1896. The Ashanti turned down an unofficial offer to become a British protectorate in 1891, extending to 1894. The British also wanted to establish a British residence in Kumasi. The Ashanti King Prempeh I refused to surrender his sovereignty. The Ashanti sent a delegation to London offering concessions on its gold trade and submission to the crown. The British, however, had already made their minds up on a military solution; they were on their way, the delegation only returning to Kumasi a few days before the troops marched in.

Colonel Sir Francis Scott left Cape Coast with the main expeditionary force of British and West Indian troops, Maxim guns and 75mm artillery in December 1895 and, travelling along the remnants of the 1874 road arrived in Kumasi in January 1896. Major Robert Baden-Powell led a native levy of several local tribes in the campaign. The Asantehene directed the Ashanti not to resist, but casualties from sickness among the British troops were high. Not a shot had been fired, but 18 Europeans died, and 50% of the troops were sick. Among the dead was Queen Victoria's son-in-law, Prince Henry of Battenberg. In 1897, Ashanti territory became a British protectorate.

Soon, Governor William Maxwell arrived in Kumasi as well. Asantehene Agyeman Prempeh was unable or unwilling to pay the 50,000 ounces of gold, so he was arrested and deposed. He was forced to sign a protection treaty and exiled to the Seychelles with other Ashanti leaders.

Prempeh I spent time in his villa on Mahe, the largest of Seychelles in the Indian Ocean. The villa was formerly a huge plantation covered with coconut trees, mango, breadfruit and orange trees, and a two-story villa. Prempeh tried to educate himself in English and ensure the children received an education.

The King Asantehene Prempeh I once stated, “My Kingdom of Ashanti will never commit itself to any such policy of protection; Ashanti people and the Kingdom of Ashanti must remain an independent sovereign state as of old, and at the same time be friends with all white men”.

The Deported King Prempeh of Asante and his attendants.
Source: Base; Mission Book

Fifth War or “War of the Golden Stool”

In the War of the Golden Stool (1900), the British representative, Sir Frederick Mitchell Hodgson, committed a political error by insisting he should sit on the Golden Stool, not understanding that it was the Royal throne and very sacred to the Ashanti.

Hodgson advanced toward Kumasi with a small force of British soldiers and local levies, arriving on March 25 1900. As a representative of a powerful nation, Hodgson was accorded traditional honours upon entering the city with children singing "God Save the Queen" to Lady Hodgson. After ascending a platform, he made a speech to the assembled Ashanti leaders. The speech, or the closest surviving account that comes through an Ashanti translator, reportedly read:

"*Your King Prempeh I is in exile and will not return to Ashanti. The Representative of the Queen of Britain will take over his power and authority. The terms of the 1874 Peace Treaty of Fomena, which required you to pay for the cost of the 1874 war, have not been forgotten. You have to pay with interest the sum of £160,000 a year. Then there is the matter of the Golden Stool of Ashanti. The Queen is entitled to the Stool; she must receive it.*

Where is the Golden Stool? I am the representative of Paramount Power. Why have you relegated me to this ordinary chair? Why did you not take the opportunity of my coming to Kumasi to bring the Golden Stool for me to sit upon?"

The speech was received in silence by the assembly, but the chiefs that were present began war preparations upon their return to their homes. Hodgson ordered a search be done for the Stool. Enraged by this act, the Ashanti attacked the soldiers engaged in the search. In his book "The Golden Stool: Some Aspects of the Conflict of Cultures in Modern Africa", the anthropologist Reverend Edwin W. Smith wrote of this: "A singularly foolish speech is an excellent example of the blunders that are made through ignorance of the African mind!".

Gaurav Desai quotes this passage and goes on to clarify that the Stool was not seen as a mere physical object and symbol of power but as a metaphysical and spiritual representation of the soul of the Ashanti people as a whole — this misunderstanding being the catalyst for the conflict, coming at a time of already strained relations.

The enraged populace produced a large number of volunteers. Yaa Asantewaa, the Queen-Mother of Ejisu, led the rebellion. In her war speech Queen Mother Yaa Asantewaa rallied resistance against the British: *"Now I have seen that some of you fear to go forward to fight for our king. If it were in the brave days, ..., chiefs would not sit down to see their king taken away without firing a shot. No foreigner could have dared to speak to a chief of the Ashanti in the way the Governor spoke to you chiefs this morning. Is it true that the bravery of the Ashanti is no more? I cannot believe it. It cannot be! I must say this if you, the men of Ashanti, will not go forward, then we will. We, the women, will. I shall call upon my fellow women. We will fight! We will fight till the last of us falls on the battlefields."* She collected men to form a force to attack the British and retrieve the exiled king.

An Akan stool believed to be for a Queen mother. Source Wikipedia

The Ashanti territories became part of the Gold Coast colony on January 1, 1902, on the condition that the Golden Stool would not be violated by British or other non-Akan foreigners

As Hodgson's deputy, Captain Cecil Armitage searched for the Stool in a nearby brush; his force was surrounded and ambushed, but a sudden rainstorm allowed the survivors to retreat to the British offices in Kumasi. The British retreated to a small enclosure, eight Europeans, dozens of mixed-race colonial administrators, and 500 Nigerian Hausas with six small field guns and four Maxim guns defended themselves. A rescue party of 700 arrived in June. The healthier men escaped, including Hodgson and his wife, and 100 Hausas returned to the coast. The remaining Ashanti court not exiled to Seychelles had mounted the offensive against the British and Fanti troops residing at the Kumasi Fort.

The Ashanti claimed a victory as they had not lost their sacred Stool. The British and their allies suffered 1,070 fatalities, and the Ashanti casualties are estimated at around 2,000. The sacred golden Stool, depicted on the Ashanti flag, had been well hidden and only discovered by road workers by accident in 1920. King Prempeh I returned from exile in 1924, travelling to Kumasi by a special train. "Thousands of white and black people fled to the beach to welcome him.

The Ashante rebellion lasted for several months, with the Asante using guerrilla tactics to attack British outposts and disrupt British supply lines. The British responded brutally, burning villages and killing both combatants and non-combatants. The British suppressed the rebellion, but not before it had caused significant loss of life and property.

The impact of the Asante Rebellion was far-reaching. It demonstrated the strength of Asante's resistance to colonial rule and the willingness of the people to fight for their independence. It also highlighted the brutality of British colonialism and the lengths to which the British were willing to go to assert their dominance.

The rebellion remains an important symbol of resistance to colonialism in Ghana and a reminder of the ongoing struggles for independence and self-determination worldwide.

The abolition of the trans-Atlantic slave trade in the 19th Century significantly impacted Ghana. The trade was a significant source of revenue for many coastal kingdoms, and its end led to a decline in their wealth and power. However, the abolition of slavery also led to the British colonisation of the Gold Coast.

During 1830–44, under the leadership of George Maclean, the British merchants began to assume an informal protectorate over the Fante states. The British Colonial Office finally agreed to take over the British forts, and in 1850 it bought out the Danes.

2. Colonial

This Chapter explores in detail the beginning and the impact of colonialism on Ghana.

Before the 1700s, the British Empire and other European powers' settlements were restricted to the coast of Africa. They could not establish colonies in Africa because of the health threat posed by malaria and yellow fever in the heart of Africa. Only one in ten Europeans survived malaria and yellow fever. During this period, the Europeans called Africa the "White Man's Grave."

However, some factors happened at the turn of the 1800s that enabled the colonisation of Africa by the Europeans. Firstly, the discovery of quinine against malaria allowed the European powers to move inland and settle down within the continent. Secondly, Europeans started sending explorers, like David Livingston and Henry Stanley Morgan, to Africa, recording and sending information about the continent's wealth to their financiers, who began to elicit more interest in the continent.

Thirdly, the innovation of the steam engine and iron-hulled boats enabled Europeans to explore the inland part of the continent through rivers. For example, Mungo Park explored the rivers Niger and Benue. Fourthly, European powers were in political competition, each country trying to assert dominance. Instead of fighting each other for European lands, they decided they should take as much land as they wanted in Africa.

Finally, the end of the slave trade created a financial vacuum that capitalists were desperate to fill. Therefore, when explorers reported the discovery of raw materials on the continent, capitalists saw an opportunity for a new "legal" trade. The Europeans also wanted to use the African population for marketing their manufactured goods.

Colonialism in Africa began in the late 19th Century, with European powers dividing the continent into territories and imposing their political and economic systems on the indigenous populations.

The Berlin Conference of 1884-1885 formalised this process, with European powers meeting to divide up the continent amongst themselves without any input from African people or their leaders.

The impact of colonialism on Africa was significant and far-reaching. One of the most significant impacts was the imposition of European political systems on African societies. The European powers created political structures that suited their interests without regard for the diverse ethnic and cultural makeup of African societies. This led to the imposition of arbitrary boundaries that divided ethnic groups and created conflict between them.

The British colonisation of Ghana began with the establishment of the Gold Coast Colony. The British had already established trading posts along the coast of present-day Ghana in the 15th Century. But, it was not until the late 19th Century that they began to exert more direct control over the region.

The British established their control over Ghana through military conquest and diplomacy. They signed treaties with local chiefs and kingdoms, often giving the British control over trade and other economic activities in the region. They also used force to subdue any resistance to their rule.

One of the key figures in the British colonisation of Ghana was Sir Frederick Hodgson, who served as Governor of the Gold Coast from 1900 to 1906. Hodgson implemented policies to consolidate British control over the region, such as introducing indirect rule. This system allowed local chiefs to maintain some autonomy in their areas but required them to carry out British policies and collect taxes for the British government. This system helped reduce the administration cost for the British and allowed them to maintain control over the region.

But the reality was that colonialism in Africa was economic exploitation. European powers sought to extract as much wealth as possible from Africa to Europe, leading to the establishment of industries that served the interests of the colonisers.

Colonialism had a significant impact on African culture and identity. European powers sought to impose their cultural values on African societies, leading to the erosion of traditional African culture and the imposition of European languages and religions. This had a lasting impact on African identity, with many Africans today struggling to reconcile their traditional cultural heritage with the legacy of colonialism.

The British established a system of colonial administration with a governor and a colonial bureaucracy. This bureaucracy also promoted the expansion of cocoa farming on the Gold Coast, which became a major source of revenue for both the British government and local farmers. This encouraged farmers to switch from traditional crops, such as cassava and potatoes, to Cocoa, which had a higher market value. This helped to boost the Gold Coast's economy and laid the foundation for Ghana's modern agricultural sector.

The British also played a role in developing infrastructure in Ghana, building roads, railways, and other forms of transportation that facilitated the movement of goods and people. However, these projects were often designed to serve the needs of the colonial economy rather than the local population and were accompanied by the exploitation of natural resources and the displacement of local communities.

One of the most significant impacts of British colonisation was the introduction of Christianity and Western education to Ghana. Missionary organisations, supported by the British colonial government, established schools and churches throughout the country, which helped to spread European values and beliefs. While this profoundly impacted Ghanaian society, it also led to the erosion of traditional cultural practices and the loss of indigenous knowledge.

2.1. COCOA IS GHANA

The Europeans made many colonial efforts to establish the commercial cultivation of Cocoa in Ghana before Tetteh Quarshie, but they all failed.

Historically, the Dutch first attempt to cultivate the crop was as early as 1815 along the then Gold Coast's coastal areas, but it was unsuccessful. In 1858, the Basel Missionaries also introduced Cocoa and coffee from Surinam. Both crops were planted at Akropong, with coffee surviving while cocoa plantations died out with time.

Another individual associated with introducing Cocoa to Ghana is Sir William Bradford Griffith, a former Governor of the Gold Coast. He experimented with the cocoa seed from Sao Tome in 1886. With the best botanist he brought from England, he raised the seedlings of Cocoa at the Aburi Botanical

Gardens and distributed them to local farmers. However, like the Basel missionaries, nothing of his effort went beyond the experimental stage.

While this happened, Tetteth Quarshie trained as a blacksmith with the Basel missionaries. He heard about the importance of this elusive crop and how it could revolutionise the earning of farmers in Ghana if it could be cultivated. He successfully graduated as a skilful Blacksmith. He was also a farmer, cultivating crops to complement his wages as a Blacksmith.

Tetteh Quarshie heard about an opportunity for a skilful blacksmith at Fernando Po in Equatorial Guinea to help shape tools and implements required to cultivate cocoa plantations.

While in Equatorial Guinea, he learned how to make the best tools and equipment for cultivating cocoa plantations. He also paid close attention to the details required to successfully cultivate Cocoa from seedlings, nursery, planting, and propagating cocoa seedlings. Tetteh also used his experience as a farmer in Ghana to understand what the European scientist and missionaries were doing back home that undermined cocoa cultivation.

After seven years in Equatorial Guinea, he invested in the best cocoa seed of the golden pod that suits the Ghana farming terrain on his way back to Ghana, a variety that he believed had a high chance of growing on a plantation in Ghana, which he planted on his family farm in the country's Eastern region. At first, Quarshie faced challenges in cultivating Cocoa, as the plant was not native to Ghana, and he had to experiment with different planting methods and care for the trees. However, over time, Quarshie developed successful cocoa plantations on his farm, named "Mampong", after the town in Fernando Po, where he had obtained the cocoa pods.

Quarshie also began to share his knowledge of cocoa farming and the seedlings with other farmers in the area, encouraging them to plant cocoa trees and showing them how to care for the crops. In the following decades, cocoa farming became a major industry in Ghana, becoming one of the world's leading cocoa producers.

Mural painting of Tetteh Quarshie (1842-1892). Source: Wikipedia

As the dominant cash crop in Ghana, Cocoa has contributed significantly to the economy's growth. Ghana's first recorded cocoa export was in 1885. Twenty years following this, in 1911, Ghana became the world's leading cocoa producer. For many parts of the twentieth Century, Ghana occupied this position. The country's position on the world market generated much revenue for the government of Gold Coast and the colonial power, Britain, in particular.

Today, Quarshie is celebrated as a national hero in Ghana for his role in introducing Cocoa to the country and promoting the development of the cocoa industry. His family farm, now known as the Tetteh Quarshie Cocoa Farm, has been preserved as a national monument and is open to visitors, who can see the original cocoa trees planted by Quarshie over 140 years ago.

The story of Tetteh Quarshie and his establishment of cocoa plantations in Ghana is a testament to the ingenuity and perseverance of the Ghanaian people, who have transformed a foreign crop into a major source of revenue and a symbol of their national identity.

During the colonial period, the British introduced policies to promote cocoa farming expansion in Ghana. Sir Frederick Hodgson, Governor of the Gold Coast from 1900 to 1906, played a key role in promoting cocoa farming, encouraging farmers to switch from traditional crops such as palm oil to Cocoa, which had a higher market value. Ghana rose to become the leading producer of Cocoa in the world, eclipsing all other cash crops in the country. As a major employer of labour and source of income to many Ghanaians, cocoa production in the country contributed about 30-40% of total output. The impact of the overwhelming growth of the cocoa industry permeated almost every aspect of Ghanaian life. It contributed largely to the growth of the money economy at the turn of the nineteenth Century. British silver coins came into wide circulation and brought into being the need for monetary and banking services. In answer to such needs, a Commercial Bank of West Africa was established with headquarters in Sierra Leone in 1882, a Savings Bank Ordinance in 1887, and the establishment of the British Bank of West Africa was established in 1994..

However, the cocoa industry also faced challenges, including fluctuations in global cocoa prices and spreading diseases such as black pod and swollen shoot disease. In response to these challenges, the Ghanaian government established the Ghana

Cocoa Board in 1947 to regulate the cocoa industry and support cocoa farmers. The Cocoa Marketing Board was also established to control cocoa export and ensure farmers received fair crop prices.

2.2. GOLD COAST INVOLVEMENT IN WORLD WAR II

Following the United Kingdom's declaration of war on Germany, the British called for the support of the African colonies to defend the Empire from brute force, bad faith, injustice, oppression and persecution from Germany. It was like the pot calling the kettle black. The British were guilty of the same thing they had accused Germany for the last 400 years. They gladly inflicted brute force, bad faith, injustice, oppression, and persecution on Africans in their African colony.

In response to critical manpower shortages following the invasion of Europe by the Nazis, Britain began to look to their colonies for supplies of able-bodied fighting men to help construct airfields, harbours, and roads. These men included combatants, military labourers, and specialist units.

Over a million African soldiers fought for colonial powers in World War II. African colonies were drawn into a war that was not theirs. From 1939, hundreds of thousands of West African soldiers were sent to the battlefront in Europe. Countless men from the British colonies had to serve as bearers and in other non-combatant roles.

African kings like the Asantehene of the Gold Coast became indispensable resources in this effort because not only had Ashante soldiers proved valiant in the earlier Ashanti British war, but their kings could also mobilise their subjects to support the British in this project. In the first few years of the war, Ghana (then known as the Gold Coast) was also an important source of raw materials such as gold, timber, and Cocoa, which were vital for the British war machine. Ghanaian women were crucial in extracting and processing these resources, often under difficult and dangerous conditions. Thousands of Ghanaians volunteered to fight in the British armed forces, serving in various theatres of the war, including North Africa, Italy, and Burma. Ghanaian soldiers played an important role in many key battles, and their bravery and sacrifice were widely recognised.

During the war, the colonial government developed several schemes to retain foreign exchange and ensure the supply of commodities necessary for a war effort. In 1939, the Home Office strongly encouraged Ghanaian farmers to produce raw materials such as rubber and palm oil and the miners to increase their output. The colonial administration also set up the Ghana Supply Board to regulate trade, manage production, and control the distribution of imports and foodstuffs.

Ghanaian women were critical in collecting the harvests of Ghana's most significant crop export: Cocoa. Due to economic difficulties, farmers were forced to produce cash crops instead of food for the duration of the war. At the outbreak of war, the colonial government prohibited cocoa exports to Germany, depriving them of critical wartime goods. The British government became the sole purchaser of all of Ghanain's cash crops and lowered the cash crop prices to cope with wartime demands.

As in many places throughout WWII, Ghana experienced an acute food shortage for six years, from 1939 to 1945. Rationing was introduced and lasted as late as 1948 in some parts of the country. A ration card was required to procure essential items, like salt, flour, butter, or tinned milk.

The Home Office was cautious not to send African soldiers to Europe as it would risk exposing them to radical political ideas that could eventually destabilise British rule in Africa. Therefore, from 1942 onward, African forces were sent to South-East Asia to repel Japanese forces. West Africa alone contributed over 250,000 men to the Second World War, and 65,000 of the 4th Gold Coast Infantry Brigade drove the Japanese out of Burma. Today, in testament to that history, the military section of Accra, Ghana's capital, is called Burma Camp, and there is also a Myohaung Barracks at Takoradi.

During the war, the African soldiers came into close contact with European soldiers on equal terms, not as masters. This war exposed the vulnerability of Europeans as prisoners of war or fighters at the front. A former colonial soldier put it like this. "In war, we saw the white men naked, crying, and we have not forgotten that picture." "The African soldiers saw their so-called masters from Europe lying in mud and filth during the war. They saw them suffering and dying", says German journalist Karl Rössel and that changed African awareness and later their political activity back home. "They realised that there are no differences between humans," he said. This led to many former soldiers joining independence movements in their home countries.

Unfortunately, many African soldiers returning to Gold Coast after the war received little official congratulations for their involvement. Upon completing the Allieds' objectives in Burma, African troops were not included in the victory speech by commanding officer General William Slim.

The role of Ghana during the war was not without controversy. Some Ghanaians saw the war as an opportunity to push for greater autonomy and independence from British rule. But the British were often reluctant to grant concessions to their colonial subjects and were accused of exploiting Ghana's resources and workforce for their own ends.

Despite these tensions, Ghana's contributions to the war effort were significant and helped to cement the country's reputation as an important player on the world stage. The war also helped to fuel nationalist sentiment in Ghana, as many Ghanaians came to believe that they deserved greater recognition and autonomy for their contributions to the war effort.

The ever-increasing assimilation of European ways by the people on the Gold Coast had already made possible the introduction of government bodies, such as a legislative council (1850) and a supreme court (1853).

Resistance to British rule included strikes and boycotts by workers and traders, who objected to the exploitation and oppression they experienced under colonialism. In 1948, a group of veterans and trade unionists formed the United Gold Coast Convention, which demanded greater political representation for Ghanaians and eventual independence. This movement laid the groundwork for establishing the Convention People's Party, led by Kwame Nkrumah, which would lead Ghana to independence in 1957.

3. Ghana's Independence

During World War II, the Gold Coast Regiment sent 65,000 troops to fight for Britain; at least 15,000 lost their lives in battle. The Gold Coast Regiment had fought for Britain in East Africa, Burma, and the Gambia. Many believed that the service of people from the Gold Coast during the war for the British government helped grant Ghana independence after the war. This seemed even more likely because countries that had been allies of Britain during World War II, such as the USA and the Soviet Union, supported giving British colonies their independence after the war.

At the end of World War II in 1945, the troops from the Gold Coast Regiment returned to the Gold Coast, now known as Ghana, after fighting for Britain. However, the Gold Coast did not get its independence. Instead, soldiers returned to the Gold Coast to high levels of unemployment and increased taxes. By this time, British rule made the Gold Coast people increasingly frustrated.

Ghana's struggle for independence was a long and complex process from the 1940s until 1957.

In 1947, the United Gold Coast Convention Party (UGCC) was set up by a group known as the Big Six. It aimed to achieve independence from Britain.

A portrait of the Big Six. Source Ghana banknotes

The Big Six were six leaders of the United Gold Coast Convention (UGCC), one of the leading political parties in the British colony of the Gold Coast, known after independence as Ghana. They were considered the founding fathers of present-day Ghana. The British colonial authorities detained them in 1948 following disturbances that led to the killing of three World War II veterans. They are pictured on the front of the Ghana cedi notes. The members of the Big Six were:

- Kwame Nkrumah – the first prime minister and first president of Ghana
- Ebenezer Ako-Adjei – founding member of the UGCC
- Edward Akufo-Addo – founding member of the UGCC and subsequently chief justice and president of Ghana

- Joseph Boakye Danquah — founding member of the UGCC
- Emmanuel Obetsebi-Lamptey — founding member of the UGCC
- William OforiAtta — founding member of the UGCC [10]

One of the key figures in Ghana's struggle for independence was Kwame Nkrumah, who became the leader of the country's independence movement in the early 1950s. Kwame Nkrumah was a political organiser who had studied in Britain and the USA and returned to Ghana to accept the position of General Secretary of the UGCC. This was the first political party formed by the local people within the colony, and it was a significant step towards self-government.

The independence movement in Ghana gained momentum with a series of protests, strikes, and boycotts that pressured the British colonial authorities. The most notable of these protests were the 1948 Accra riots.

Of the 54,000 Gold Coast Regiment troops returning home from World War II, more than 53,000 were still unemployed. On February 28 1948, a group of unarmed former soldiers joined to protest peacefully. They asked the Governor of the Gold Coast for the payment they had been promised for their contribution to the war. The British officials stopped the protesters and fired openly into the crowd. Three veterans were killed instantly: Sergeant Adjetey, Corporal Attipoe, and Private Odartey Lamptey.

Riots broke out immediately, and the UGCC demanded that the British set up a new government led by Africans if they wanted to stop the riots. The riots continued for another five days, shops and stores were looted, and more deaths occurred. The riots ended with the arrest of the UGCC leaders and Britain's introduction of the new Riot Act.

The Accra riots marked a turning point in the independence struggle, as they brought the issue of Ghana's independence to the forefront of the international stage. The British were also under pressure from international allies such as the USA, so they were forced to allow this political party to form peacefully.

However, the UGCC soon became divided over the issue of how to achieve independence, with some members favouring a more gradualist approach. In contrast, others advocated for a more radical and aggressive strategy. Nkrumah believed that Ghana's destiny was in its own hands and that it was time for the country to break free from British colonialism.

By 1949, Nkrumah clarified that he thought the UGCC was not doing enough to push for independence. Nkrumah was worried that the other members of the Big Six would agree to something less than full self-government through the new constitution. He set up the Convention People's Party (CPP), through which he called for a national strike. Nkrumah's famous slogan was, "Seek ye first the political kingdom, and all other things shall be added unto you." This became the rallying cry of Ghana's independence movement. The Convention People's Party (CPP) in 1949 became Ghana's dominant political force, leading the country to independence in 1957.

Initially, Nkrumah's goal was to use non-violent protests under the slogan 'Self Government Now!' to achieve independence in the Gold Coast's immediate future. Despite calling for peaceful protest, Nkrumah was blamed when the protests turned violent, and he was arrested and sentenced to three years in prison.

The CPP adopted a more militant approach to the struggle for independence, with mass protests, strikes, and boycotts that pressured the British colonial authorities. The most notable of these protests was the 1950s' Positive Action campaign, which called for a boycott of British goods and services and aimed to bring the colonial economy to a standstill. The campaign successfully brought international attention to the struggle for independence in Ghana and helped lay the groundwork for the country's eventual independence in 1957.

Nkrumah was supported by people like Mabel Dove Danquah, who would become the first woman elected to the Legislative Assembly of the Gold Coast in 1954.

Mabel Dove Danquah. Source *bbc.com*

Following World War II, Britain became involved in the Cold War. However, the British government was worried that if they did not respond to the ongoing protests and allow a democratic election in the Gold Coast, the leaders might ally with the communist Soviet Union to get the desired election. This would be a huge loss for Britain as they would lose an African ally.

In 1951 the British government agreed to hold national elections on the Gold Coast. The CPP won 34 out of 38 seats, and Nkrumah was made leader of the Gold Coast Colony. With this new position, he demanded independence again in 1956. Negotiations with the British government followed, and on March 6, 1957, Ghana became the first sub-Saharan African country to gain independence, with Nkrumah as its Prime Minister. Ghanaian Independence Day has been celebrated on March 6 every year since.

3.1. KWAME NUKRUMAH'S SPEECH ON INDEPENDENCE DAY: "I SPEAK OF FREEDOM."

Date: March 6 1957

Fellow citizens of Ghana,

I am glad to be able to speak to you tonight on this historic occasion, the Independence Day of Ghana. This is an event that has been long awaited and much desired, not only by the people of Ghana, but by the millions of Africans who are anxious to see the speedy liberation of their continent from the bondage of colonialism.

We are gathered here tonight to mark the end of an era, the end of the period of colonialism in Africa. We are gathered here to celebrate the birth of a new nation, the nation of Ghana.

This is a great day in the history of Africa and a great day in the history of the world. It is a day when a new nation is born with the potential to be great, a nation that can show the world what can be achieved when men and women of different races and religions come together in a spirit of brotherhood and cooperation.

We have a great task ahead of us. We must build a nation that is strong and united, a nation that is prosperous and free. We must create a society in which every man, woman, and child can live in peace and security and in which every person can fully develop the talents and abilities with which he or she has been endowed.

We must create a society in which there is no discrimination, no exploitation, no oppression. We must create a society in which there is freedom of speech, freedom of the press, freedom of worship, and freedom from fear.

We must create a society where there is justice for all, and the rule of law is respected. We must create a society where the nation's resources are used for the benefit of all, not just for the benefit of a privileged few.

We must strive to achieve these ideals, and we must do so with all our strength and determination. We must be prepared to make sacrifices, work hard, face difficulties and setbacks, and overcome them.

But I am confident that we can do this. I am confident that we can build a great nation that will be a beacon of hope for all the peoples of Africa and the oppressed peoples of the world.

Fellow citizens of Ghana, let us go forward with courage and determination, knowing that the road ahead will not be easy but that the goal we seek is noble and just. Let us work together as one people to build a new Ghana, a Ghana that will be free, prosperous, and great.

Thank you.

The struggle for independence in Ghana was not without its challenges and a series of setbacks and obstacles, including violence, repression, and political divisions, marked it. However, it ultimately achieved its goals and helped inspire other independence movements across the continent and worldwide.

Today, Ghana's struggle for independence remains an important chapter in the country's and the continent's history. It continues to be celebrated as a symbol of the country's resilience, determination, and commitment to self-determination and national sovereignty.

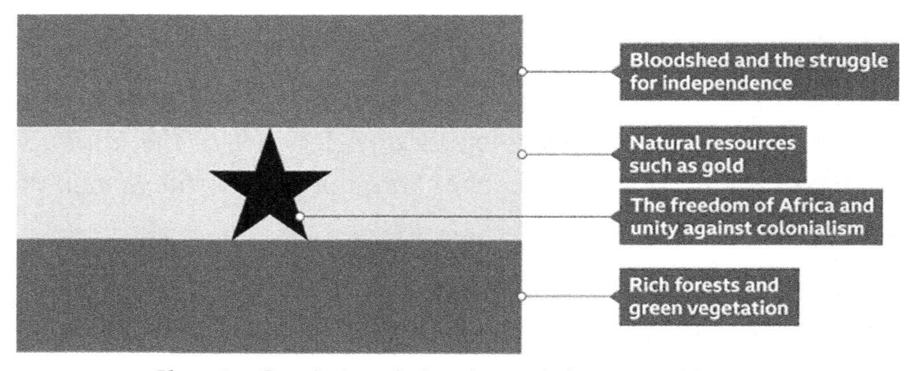

Ghanaian flag designed Theodosia Okoh. Source: *bbc.com*

3.2. WHY GHANA WAS THE FIRST AFRICAN COUNTRY TO GAIN NATIONAL INDEPENDENCE

While most historians would disagree that Ghana became independent because of one person or group, many would argue that Ghana won its independence because many people worked together and took advantage of the circumstances to achieve their goals.

Ghana's independence on March 6, 1957, was a significant milestone in the history of Africa. It marked the first time a sub-Saharan African nation had achieved independence from colonial rule. This historic achievement was not a coincidence but the result of a unique combination of factors.

One of the significant factors was the coming together of the Big Six In 1947 to form the United Gold Coast Convention party (UGCC) aimed to achieve independence from Britain.

Secondly, the visionary leadership of Kwame Nkrumah believed in the African people's potential to govern themselves. He was an intellectual and skilled organiser who used the frustration after the war and the growing Pan-African movement to build up the support of Ghanaians around the idea of independence. He used his position as the United Gold Coast Convention (UGCC) leader to mobilise the masses and challenge British rule.

Thirdly, women's role in supporting and spreading the message of independence cannot be overemphasised. For example, Mabel Dove Danquah used her experience as a journalist and newspaper editor to share her views on independence. She regularly wrote in The Times of West Africa, one of the Gold Coast's first newspapers. Danquah became a major supporter of the CPP and recruited many women to their cause.

The fourth factor was the unity of the people of Ghana. The struggle for independence was not just the work of one man but a collective effort by Ghanaians from all walks of life. The political elite, workers, farmers, and students were all involved in the struggle. This unity was built on a shared sense of national identity and a common desire for freedom.

Fifth, the global political climate of the time was also in Ghana's favour. After the Second World War, the British government could not afford to keep suppressing protests after the huge cost of World War II. The Cold War meant that Britain had to compromise to avoid the Gold Coast becoming a communist ally.

During this period, the international community was increasingly sympathetic to the cause of African independence movements. The United Nations Charter, which was signed in 1945, recognised the right of all peoples to self-determination. This principle provided a strong legal and moral foundation for Ghana's struggle for independence. The UN played an instrumental role in facilitating negotiations between the British colonial government and Ghanaian nationalists and also provided financial and technical assistance to the country during the post-independence period.

The peaceful nature of Ghana's independence struggle was also significant. Unlike other African countries that achieved independence through violence, Ghana's independence was achieved through non-violent means. This approach helped to earn the international community's support and avoid the chaos that often accompanies violent uprisings.

Finally, Ghana's attainment of independence was also facilitated by the strategic position of the country. Ghana was a hub for commerce and transportation in West Africa. The country had a vibrant economy that was closely tied to Britain. The British recognised the importance of Ghana's economy and were willing to negotiate a peaceful transfer of power to ensure regional stability.

These are important lessons that African countries must learn as they move from independence to becoming developed countries.

In conclusion, Ghana's attainment of independence resulted from a combination of factors, including visionary leadership, unity, global political climate, peaceful struggle, and strategic position. These factors made Ghana the first African country to achieve national independence, paving the way for other African countries to follow suit. Ghana's independence marked the beginning of a new era in African history, where the people of Africa were free to govern themselves and chart their own destiny.

3.3. THE ORIGIN OF NKRUMAH'S PHILOSOPHY

Kwame Nkrumah, a prominent figure in African history and a leading advocate for Pan-Africanism, developed a philosophy that was deeply rooted in the African experience and influenced by various intellectual and political currents of his time. Nkrumah's philosophy can be traced back to several key sources that shaped his thinking and provided the foundation for his vision of African liberation and unity.

Pan-Africanism – One of the central pillars of Nkrumah's philosophy was Pan-Africanism. This movement sought to unite Africans across the continent and in the diaspora and reclaim African agency and sovereignty. Nkrumah drew inspiration from Pan-African leaders, such as Marcus Garvey and W.E.B. Du Bois, who advocated for the unity and liberation of people of African descent worldwide. Nkrumah's exposure to Pan-Africanist ideas during his studies in the United States and the United Kingdom deeply influenced his thinking and became a cornerstone of his philosophy.

Nationalism and Anti-Colonialism – Nkrumah's philosophy also emerged from his fervent nationalism and commitment to the anti-colonial struggle. Growing up in the Gold Coast (present-day Ghana) under British colonial rule, Nkrumah witnessed first-hand the injustices and inequalities perpetuated by colonial powers. His experiences shaped his deep-rooted belief in the rights of Africans to self-determination and independence. Nkrumah's nationalist sentiments and encounters with other anti-colonial thinkers, such as Jomo Kenyatta and Julius Nyerere, significantly shaped his philosophy.

Socialism and Marxism — Nkrumah's philosophy also bore the influence of socialist and Marxist ideologies. He believed that socialism offered a path towards socio-economic equality, justice, and eradicating exploitation. Nkrumah saw socialism as a means to liberate African nations from neo-colonial domination and achieve inclusive development. He incorporated socialist principles into his vision for Ghana's economic and political transformation, advocating for state-led development and equitable distribution of resources.

African Communalism and Traditional Values — Nkrumah recognized the importance of African communalism and traditional values in his philosophy. He emphasized the need for African societies to draw upon their indigenous cultural values, customs, and communal solidarity to guide the process of nation-building and development. Nkrumah believed that African societies possessed inherent strengths and wisdom that could contribute to the progress and well-being of their nations.

Intellectual Influences — Nkrumah was influenced by a range of intellectuals and philosophers, both African and non-African. He engaged with the works of African scholars, such as Leopold Senghor, Frantz Fanon, and Cheikh Anta Diop, who explored issues of identity, colonialism, and the decolonization of African minds. Nkrumah also drew upon the works of Marx, Lenin, and Mao Zedong, adapting their ideas to suit the African context.

Nkrumah saw independent Ghana as a spearhead for liberating the rest of Africa from colonial rule and establishing a socialist African unity under his leadership. Once in power, Nkrumah set out to transform Ghana into a modern, industrialised state. His ambitious plans included building roads, schools, hospitals, and factories, and he believed that Ghana's resources should be used for the benefit of its people. His famous book, "Africa Must Unite, " encapsulated his vision when he argued that Africa could only achieve true independence by working together and creating a united continent.

One of Nkrumah's most significant achievements was the introduction of the Seven-Year Development Plan in 1964, also known as the "Seven-Year Plan of Accelerated Industrial and Social Development." This plan aimed to transform Ghana into an industrialised, socialist state. It included ambitious projects, such as creating the Tema Industrial Complex and the construction of the Akosombo Dam.

Lake Volta in Ghana became the largest artificial lake in the world. It spans over 320 miles and can be seen from space. His plan was designed to be a development blueprint to bring Ghana prosperity.

After achieving independence for the public in 1960, the state became identified with a single political party (the CPP), with Nkrumah as life president, taking ever more power for himself (similar to Lee Kuan Yew, Singapore's first prime minister).

Nkrumah's ambitious plans and authoritarian style of government led to criticisms from both within Ghana and the international community. His government was accused of human rights violations, suppression of political dissent, and corruption. The economy also struggled under the weight of Nkrumah's ambitious industrialisation plans, and Ghana's debt grew significantly.

3.4. DR KWAME NKRUMAH'S VISION OF A UNITED AFRICA:

"I Speak of Freedom" Date: 24 May 1963

Your Majesties, Your Royal Highnesses, Distinguished Ladies and Gentlemen,

We have come to the end of a long journey, a journey that has taken us from the scattered tribes and kingdoms of Africa to this great gathering of the leaders of our continent. This is a historic moment, a moment that will be remembered for centuries to come, a moment that marks the birth of a new Africa.

For centuries, Africa has been divided and conquered by foreign powers. We have been exploited, oppressed, and enslaved. But today, we declare that the era of colonialism is over, and today, we declare that Africa is free.

But our freedom is not complete. We are still divided, still fragmented into small states that are weak and vulnerable to outside influence. We must unite. We must come together as one people, one nation, one Africa.

Our vision is of a United Africa, a continent that is strong and free, a continent that is prosperous and just. We envision a continent that is a leader in world affairs, a continent that speaks with one voice and commands respect and admiration.

We know that the road ahead will not be easy, and we know that there will be many obstacles to overcome and many challenges to face. But we are confident that we can overcome these obstacles and meet these challenges.

We are confident because we know that we have the support of the people of Africa and the people of the world. We know that the struggle for African unity is not just our struggle, but the struggle of all people who love freedom and justice.

We must work together as one people to build a new Africa. We must be prepared to make sacrifices, work hard, face difficulties and setbacks, and overcome them. We can do this. We can build a United Africa, a continent that is strong and free, a continent that is prosperous and just. We can build a continent that will be a beacon of hope for all the peoples of Africa and for all the oppressed peoples of the world.

Let us go forward with courage and determination, knowing that the road ahead will not be easy, but that the goal we seek is noble and just. Let us work together as one people to build a new Africa, a United Africa.

Thank you.

Kwame Nkrumah's vision for a United Africa was both ambitious and compelling. He believed that the people of Africa had a common history, culture, and destiny. By working together, they could overcome the legacy of colonialism and build a new free, prosperous, and just Africa.

At the heart of Nkrumah's vision was the idea of unity. He believed that the divisions created by colonialism were holding Africa back and that Africa could achieve its full potential only by coming together as one people, one nation. He saw the potential of a United Africa to be a leader in world affairs, to speak with one voice, and to command respect and admiration.

Nkrumah's vision was not just about political unity but also about economic and cultural unity. He believed that a United Africa could create a common market that would benefit all its people and promote cultural exchange and understanding between the different peoples of Africa.

However, Nkrumah was also realistic about the challenges that would need to be overcome to achieve his vision. He acknowledged that the road ahead would not be easy and that many obstacles would be waiting to be overcome. He called on the people of Africa to be prepared to make sacrifices, work hard, and face difficulties and setbacks.

Nkrumah's vision for a United Africa was not just a dream but a call to action. He believed that the people of Africa had the power to shape their destiny and that by working together, they could build a strong, free, prosperous, and just continent.

Today, Nkrumah's vision for a United Africa remains as relevant as ever. Africa faces many challenges, including poverty, conflict, and underdevelopment. But the idea of African unity remains a powerful force for change.

The African Union, established in 2002, is working to promote unity and cooperation among African states and addresses the continent's challenges. While progress has been slow, there have been some notable successes, such as the African Continental Free Trade Area, established in 2019 and aims to create a single market for goods and services across the continent.

In conclusion, Kwame Nkrumah's vision for a United Africa was an ambitious and compelling call to action. He believed that by working together, the people of Africa could overcome the legacy of colonialism and build a new Africa that was free, prosperous, and just. While progress has been slow, the idea of African unity remains a powerful force for change, and Nkrumah's vision continues to inspire and guide the continent.

3.5. KWAME NKRUMAH'S BOOK "NEO-COLONIALISM: THE HIGHEST STAGE OF IMPERIALISM."

In Kwame Nkrumah's book "Neo-Colonialism: The Highest Stage of Imperialism," Nkrumah examines the concept of neo-colonialism and its impact on African nations. The book is a powerful critique of the economic and political systems that perpetuate colonialism in Africa and a call to action for African leaders to break free from the chains of neo-colonialism and achieve true independence.

Nkrumah argues that neo-colonialism is the continuation of colonialism in a new form. While colonialism was characterised by direct rule by foreign powers, neo-colonialism is characterised by indirect rule through economic and political systems that are controlled by foreign powers. Nkrumah suggests that neo-colonialism is a more insidious form of imperialism, as it allows foreign powers to maintain control over African nations without the need for military occupation or overt political control.

Nkrumah's analysis focuses on the economic dimension of neo-colonialism. He argues that African nations are trapped in a system of economic dependence on foreign powers, particularly the former colonial powers of Europe. African economies are structured to perpetuate this dependence, with exports focused on raw materials and imports focused on finished goods. This system, Nkrumah argues, leads to a situation in which African nations cannot control their own economic destiny.

Nkrumah also highlights the political dimension of neo-colonialism. He argues that foreign powers control African nations using political systems and institutions. This includes supporting authoritarian leaders who are willing to collaborate with foreign powers and using international organizations like the United Nations to legitimize their influence in African nations.

Overall, Nkrumah's book is a powerful critique of neo-colonialism and a call to action for African leaders to break free from the chains of economic and political dependence on foreign powers. He argues that true independence can only be achieved through a radical transformation of African economies and political systems and a rejection of the systems of control that have perpetuated colonialism for centuries.

One of the key themes of Nkrumah's book is the importance of unity among African nations in the struggle against neo-colonialism. Nkrumah argues that African nations must work together to break free from the systems of control imposed by foreign powers and build a new economic and political order that is grounded in African values and priorities.

To achieve this goal, Nkrumah suggests that African nations must build strong regional and continental institutions that can promote economic and political integration and counterbalance the influence of foreign powers. He advocates for establishing a unified African currency, a common market, and a continental development bank, among other measures.

Nkrumah also emphasizes the need for African nations to control their resources and industries. He argues that African nations must develop their own manufacturing and industrial sectors and focus on adding value to their raw materials rather than simply exporting them. This would require a significant shift in economic policy and infrastructure a human capital investment.

Another important aspect of Nkrumah's book is his critique of Western aid and development programs. Nkrumah argues that these programs are often designed to perpetuate neo-colonialism rather than promote development in African nations. He suggests that African nations should reject aid programs with strings attached and instead focus on building their capacity to manage their own resources and economies.

In conclusion, Kwame Nkrumah's book "Neo-Colonialism: The Highest Stage of Imperialism" remains an important contribution to African political thought and a powerful call to action for African leaders and activists. Nkrumah's analysis of neo-colonialism and his vision for a new, more just economic and political order in Africa remain relevant today as African nations grapple with colonialism's legacy and the ongoing impact of foreign influence on their economies and political systems. His book remains a powerful call to action for African leaders and activists committed to achieving true independence and building a more just and equitable world.

3.6. WHY DR KWAME NKRUMAH WAS OVERTHROWN.

The first ever coup in Ghana was recorded in 1966, and its aftermath paved the way for a series of coups to follow. This section considers the reasons for the overthrow of Dr Kwame Nkrumah and the history behind the 1966 coup.

Picture of Nkrumah. Source: *manuelasare.blogspot.com*

In 1957, Ghana gained its independence and, by 1960, its total freedom by becoming a Republic, obliterating all sorts of British powers in the country, with Nkrumah now possessing the highest power of the land. In 1964, Dr Kwame Nkrumah introduced a bill to make him the most powerful leader in Ghana. Implementing the Preventive Detention Act in 1958 created the impression of Nkrumah as a dictator. The law crippled any organisation or person that would rise against him and his reign. The Nkrumah administration arrested most leaders of the UGCC who declined to support him and opposed Nkrumah's policies. This sparked mutiny and created a state of anarchy in the minds of most politicians.

As a strong Pan-Africanist, Dr. Kwame Nkrumah stood his ground in gaining other African states' independence. His passion and drive for African unity shifted his focal point from Ghana to other African states, which made him an ambitious leader. Many Ghanaians felt neglected by his focus on African unity rather than Ghana's development.

Another major reason was Dr Kwame's disregard for the Ghanaian culture and chiefs. He did not actively partake in his administration's chiefs and traditional councils, and his attitude towards traditional leaders was lacking. There was also economic hardship and the tag of corruption in his administration.

The final nail to Dr Nkrumah's overthrow was the perception by the international community that he was leaning more toward the Eastern world. Ghana and other African independence happened in the 1960s during the cold war. During the cold war, the economic nature of the world was divided into The Western and The Eastern Blocks. The United States of America controlled the Western world, with capitalism as its major economic system. At the same time, Russia controlled the Eastern Block, with Africa choosing between these two systems. President Nkrumah was a proud Socialist. This led to the change of regime plotting by the USA, which successfully led to the overthrow of Dr Kwame Nkrumah.

In February 1966, while Nkrumah was in Beijing, army and police leaders rose against him and his regime was replaced by a National Liberation Council chaired by Lieut. Gen. Joseph A. Ankrah. Nkrumah went into exile in Guinea and died there in 1972.

After Nkrumah's ousting in a coup in 1966, Ghana experienced a period of political instability and military rule. There were several military coups, with military leaders ruling the country until the 1990s. Human rights abuses, political oppression, and economic decline characterised military rule.

3.7. SERIES OF COUP IN GHANA

Lieut. Gen. Joseph A. Ankrah

During Ankrah's reign, the government machinery was overhauled and conservative financial policies were introduced. But Ankrah failed to redeem a promise to restore parliamentary democracy and in 1969 he gave way to the dynamic young brigadier Akwasi Amankwaa Afrifa, a principal leader of the coup.

A constituent assembly produced a constitution for a second republic, and a general election was held in August 1969. This resulted in a substantial victory for the Progress Party, led by Kofi Busia, a university professor who had consistently opposed Nkrumah. Busia became prime minister, and a year later, a former chief justice, Edward Akufo-Addo, was chosen president.

Edward Akufo-Addo

Akufo-Addo's civilian regime, handicapped by the great burden of foreign debt it had inherited and the lower prices obtained for cocoa on the world market, was slow to produce its expected results. In January 1972, impatient army officers intervened again and the government was taken over by a National Redemption Council (NRC) of military men chaired by Col. Ignatius Kutu Acheampong.

Col. Ignatius Kutu Acheampong

The national assembly was dissolved, public meetings prohibited, political parties proscribed, and leading politicians imprisoned. In July 1972, a retroactive Subversion Decree was enacted under which military courts were empowered to impose the death penalty for offences such as subversive political activity, robbery, theft, and damaging public property. The military regime clearly failed to maintain good order or anything resembl a prosperous or stable economy. Ghana's gross domestic product, export earnings, and living standards steeply declined.

In 1975, the NRC was reorganized to include some civilians, but ultimate power was given to a Supreme Military Council (SMC). In 1977 the SMC proposed a "Union Government to which everybody will belong," with the military sharing the government with civilians rather than political parties. But a national referendum held to approve this served mainly to show the unpopularity of the SMC.

Gen. Frederick W.K. Akuffo

Acheampong was replaced as SMC chairman by Lieut. Gen. Frederick W.K. Akuffo, was less effective in governing than his predecessor. Eventually, in 1979, as the economy floundered, the government of the generals was overthrown by young officers and non-commissioned officers, led by an air force flight lieutenant, Jerry Rawlings.

Jerry Rawlings

Acheampong and Akuffo were executed, and a quick return to the parliamentary government was organized. But Pres. Hilla Limann failed to produce the radical improvements in Ghana's political and economic life that Rawlings and his colleagues sought. At the end of 1981, Rawlings decided that he and those who thought like him must take the lead in all walks of life and again overthrow the government. His second military coup established a Provisional National Defence Council as the supreme national government; at local levels, people's defence committees were to take the campaign for national renewal down to the grassroots.

Initially, older Ghanaians doubted that Rawlings and his colleagues could provide a more effective and less self-interested government than the older politicians or generals. At the same time, other young soldiers thought they could engineer coups to secure the fruits of power. But Rawlings easily snuffed out two countercoups in 1982 and 1983, and it was apparent that there was wide and genuine approval of his purpose of reforming Ghana's political and economic life. This continued even when he decided that there was no alternative but to follow conservative economic policies—such as dropping subsidies and price controls to reduce inflation, privatizing many state-owned companies, and devaluing the currency to stimulate exports—that would secure International Monetary Fund (IMF) support and other foreign aid. These free-market measures revived Ghana's economy, which by the early 1990s had one of the highest growth rates in Africa.

3.8. GHANA'S TRANSITION OF POWER IN 2000

Ghana's transition of power in 2000 marked a significant moment in the country's democratic history. It was the first time in Ghana's fourth republic that power was transferred from one political party to another through the ballot box.

The 2000 election saw the National Democratic Congress (NDC) government led by President Jerry Rawlings face off against the New Patriotic Party (NPP) led by John Agyekum Kufuor. The election was fiercely contested, with both parties campaigning vigorously nationwide.

Local and international observers deemed the election free and fair, and the NPP emerged victorious, winning 100 seats in parliament against the NDC's 92. Kufuor was sworn in as Ghana's new president on January 7, 2001, marking a peaceful transition of power.

The transition of power in 2000 was significant because it demonstrated Ghana's commitment to democratic governance and the rule of law. The country's electoral commission played a crucial role in ensuring the fairness and transparency of the election, while both parties showed a willingness to accept the outcome of the vote.

However, the transition was not without its challenges. The NDC initially refused to concede defeat, citing irregularities in the electoral process. The party challenged the results in court but later dropped the case, paving the way for a peaceful transition of power.

Furthermore, the successful transition of power in 2000 was significant in consolidating Ghana's democratic credentials and reputation as a beacon of democracy in Africa. It paved the way for subsequent peaceful transitions of power in the country, with the opposition parties winning elections in 2008 and 2016.

The transition of power in 2000 was also significant because it departed from Ghana's military coups and authoritarian's rule history. The country had experienced several military coups since gaining independence in 1957, and the transition in 2000 marked a shift towards democratic governance and civilian rule.

The role of civil society organizations, the media, and the international community in ensuring a free and fair election cannot be overstated. These actors played a crucial role in monitoring the electoral process, ensuring that it was conducted transparently and responsibly. The media provided extensive election coverage, which helped inform voters and hold political parties accountable.

In conclusion, Ghana's transition of power in 2000 was a significant moment in its democratic history, marking a departure from its history of military coups and authoritarian rule. Successfully transferring power from one political party to another demonstrated Ghana's commitment to democratic governance and the rule of law.

3.9. JERRY RAWLINS OF GHANA

Jerry John Rawlings, born on June 22, 1947, was a Ghanaian military officer and politician who served as the country's President from 1981 to 2001. He played a significant role in

Ghana's political history, particularly in the country's transition from military rule to democratic governance.

Jerry Rawlins. Source: nation.Africa

Rawlings first came to prominence in Ghana in 1979 when he led a successful military coup that ousted the government of General Frederick Akuffo. Rawlings established the Armed Forces Revolutionary Council (AFRC) and assumed the role of Chairman, promising to return Ghana to democratic rule within a few months.

However, in 1981, Rawlings overthrew the AFRC and established the Provisional National Defence Council (PNDC), a military government. Rawlings maintained that the PNDC was necessary to deal with Ghana's economic and social problems and to ensure a peaceful transition to democracy.

Under Rawlings' leadership, Ghana underwent significant economic and social reforms. The government instituted economic policies to stabilize the economy and address inflation, unemployment, and poverty. Rawlings also pursued social reforms, including education and healthcare initiatives, that sought to improve the lives of ordinary Ghanaians.

Rawlings' rule was not without controversy. His government was accused of human rights abuses, including extra-judicial killings and torture of political opponents. Rawlings, however, maintained that such measures were necessary to maintain stability and security in Ghana.

1992 Rawlings transitioned Ghana to democratic governance and won the presidential elections that year. He was re-elected in 1996, and his government oversaw significant improvements in Ghana's democratic institutions, including establishing an independent electoral commission.

Rawlings was known for his charisma and strong personality and was widely respected in Ghana and abroad. He played an influential role in African politics, particularly in West Africa, and was involved in resolving conflicts and promoting peace in the region.

Rawlings' leadership legacy in Ghana remains contested. While some view him as a hero who led the country through a difficult period and laid the foundation for Ghana's current democratic governance, others see him as a controversial figure whose rule was marked by authoritarianism and human rights abuses.

Rawlings died on November 12, 2020, at the age of 73. His death was widely mourned in Ghana and across Africa, with many honouring him for his contributions to the country and the region.

Many Ghanaians credit Rawlings with laying the foundation for Ghana's democratic governance and economic growth in the 21st century. His efforts to combat corruption and promote accountability set a precedent for future leaders. His commitment to social programs helped reduce poverty and improve the lives of ordinary Ghanaians.

3.10. THE REPRESENTATION OF WOMEN IN POLITICS AND LEADERSHIP IN GHANA

In recent years, Ghana has made significant strides in promoting gender equality and women's representation in politics and leadership positions. Historically, women in Ghana have been excluded from political and leadership positions due to cultural and traditional beliefs that view women as inferior to men. However, in 1960, the first woman, Esther Ocloo, was appointed to the Council of State by Ghana's first President, Kwame Nkrumah. Since then, Ghana has witnessed a steady increase in women holding political and leadership positions.

In 1992, Ghana's Fourth Republican Constitution guaranteed women's equal representation in politics and the country implemented a quota system to ensure women's participation in decision-making. The quota system requires political parties to reserve at least 30% of their parliamentary seats for women. Implementing this quota system has resulted in significant progress, with women currently occupying approximately 14% of the seats in Ghana's parliament.

However, despite the gains made through the quota system, women's political representation remains low. Women continue to face various forms of discrimination and marginalization that hinder their ability to participate fully in politics and leadership. The lack of financial resources and limited access to education and information are some of the factors that hinder women's political participation in Ghana.

Civil society organizations (CSOs) have played a critical role in promoting gender equality and women's representation in politics and leadership in Ghana. These organizations have advocated for policies and laws promoting women's participation in decision-making. They have also provided training and support to women seeking political and leadership positions, including mentorship and networking opportunities.

4. Geography

The modern state of Ghana is named after the African empire that flourished until the 13th century. The centre of the empire of Ghana, situated close to the Sahara in western Sudan, lies about 500 miles (800 km) to the northwest of the nearest part of modern Ghana. It is reasonably certain that no part of current Ghana lies within its borders. However, modern-day Ghana was named in honour of this powerful, ancient, and independent West African civilization.

Modern-day Ghana is situated on the coast of the Gulf of Guinea in western Africa. Ghana is bordered to the northwest and north by Burkina Faso, to the east by Togo, to the south by the Atlantic Ocean, and to the west by Côte d'Ivoire.

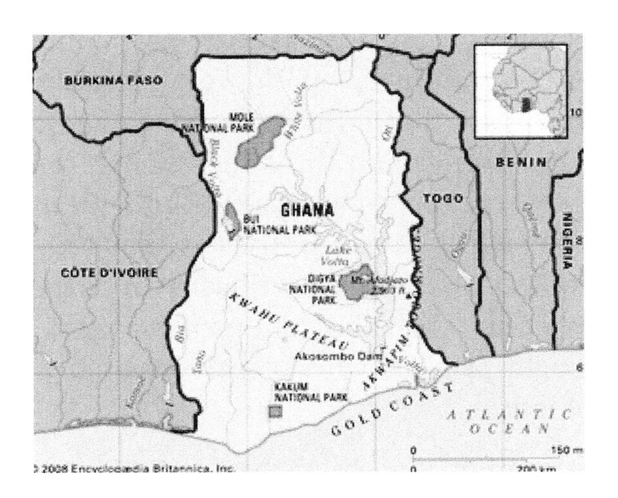

Map of Ghana. Source: *britannica.com*

The landscape in Ghana is predominantly characterized by moderate elevation, with heights generally below 3,000 feet (900 meters). Most of the country consists of clay and sandstones in which limestone strata occur. Lake Volta dominates the north-central part of the country. This artificial lake extends far into the central part of the country behind the Akosombo Dam and covers about 3,275 square miles (8,500 square km).

In the forest zone, the soils are mostly lateritic. Most of the land is fertile and less-acidic (red, brown, and yellow-brown, relatively well-drained soils) in areas of moderate precipitation exceeding 65 inches (1,650 mm) of rain. The coastal savanna zone has abundant soil types, including tropical black earth and tropical grey piles of earth. The Akuse clays fill a broad zone across the coastal savanna plains and respond well to agricultural use under irrigation and mechanical cultivation.

4.1. CLIMATE

Like the rest of the Guinea Coast, Ghana's climate is determined largely by the interplay of two air masses: a hot, dry continental air mass that forms over the Sahara and a warm, humid maritime tropical air mass that stems from the South Atlantic. Continental air moves southward with the northeast trade winds, known in western Africa as the harmattan, while maritime tropical air moves northward with the southwest trades. Rains occur when the dominant air mass is maritime tropical; drought prevails when continental air and the harmattan dominate.

In the savanna country north of the Kwahu Plateau, there are two seasons—a dry season from November to March, with hot days and cool nights under clear skies, and a wet season that peaks in August and September.

The annual mean temperature is 78 to 84 °F (26 to 29 °C); the daily range is about 43 to 46 °F (6 to 8 °C) along the coast and 45 to 63 °F (7 to 17 °C) in the north. Average relative humidities range from nearly 100% in the south to 65% in the north. However, during the harmattan season, figures as low as 12% have been recorded in the north and around Accra. Generally, the hottest months are February and March, just before the rains, and the lowest temperatures occur in January or along the coast in August.

4.2. VEGETATION

Three principal vegetation types occur from south to north the coastal savanna, the forest zone, and the northern savanna zone.

The coastal savanna in the south=eastern plains around Accra consists of a mixture of scrub and tall grass (mostly Guinea grass), with giant anthills, often 10 to 14 feet (3 to 4 metres) high, providing an anchorage for thicket clumps and fire-resistant species, such as the baobab (Adansonia digitata).

In the forest zone, the mean annual rainfall exceeds 45 inches (1,140 mm) and is well distributed throughout the year without a pronounced dry season). The predominant vegetation consists of evergreen and tropical semi-deciduous forests. There are tall trees of varying heights, forming a closed canopy at the top, above which tower a few forest giants, such as hardwood and African mahogany. The evergreen forest is in the extreme southwest, where the precipitation exceeds 65 inches (1,650 mm) a year, while there is a semi-deciduous forest farther north.

The dense forest zone formerly covered an area of about 30,000 square miles (78,000 square km), but farming activities and timber exploitation have reduced it to less than 8,000 square miles (21,000 square km), including about 6,000 square miles (15,500 square km) of reserved forest.

The northern savanna is found in the northern two-thirds of the country. The low annual precipitation, between 30 and 45 inches (760 and 1,140 mm), occurs in a single season and is followed by intense drought. The vegetation consists mostly of tall Guinea grass and a scattering of low trees, such as the shea butter tree and grassland.

Ghana is relatively rich in animal life, although it has been reduced by hunting and the spread of human settlement. Large mammals include lions, leopards, hyenas, antelope, elephants, buffalo, wild hogs, chimpanzees, and many monkeys. Among the snakes are pythons, cobras, horned and puff adders, and green mambas. Crocodiles, endangered manatees, and otters are found in the rivers and lagoons. Hippopotamuses are found in the Volta River. There are many species of lizards, tortoises, and giant snails. Among the numerous birds are parrots, hornbills, kingfishers, eagles, kites, herons, cuckoos, nightjars, sunbirds, egrets, vultures, snakebirds, and plantain eaters.

4.3. ETHNIC AND LINGUISTIC GROUPS

Many historians believe that present Ghana was a meeting place for two major trans-Saharan routes, the Niger and Sénégal rivers to Morocco and the Niger Bend and Lake Chad with Tunisia and Tripoli. There is evidence that Mande traders reached parts of modern Ghana north of the forest (seeking gold dust) by the 14th century and Hausa merchants (desiring kola nuts) by the 16th century. In this way, Ghana's inhabitants were influenced by the new wealth and cross-fertilization of ideas that arose in the great empires of western Sudan following the development of Islamic civilization in northern Africa.

The Akan-speaking peoples, who now inhabit most of the forest and coastlands, were founded about the 13th century by the Mande; other satellites were established by the 15th century by invaders from the Hausa region. In the 17th century, the founders of the Ga and Ewe states arrived from what is now Nigeria.

There are over 75 languages in Ghana, but only ten are numerically significant. The largest groups are the Akan (the Anyi, Asante, Baule, Fante, and Guang), Mole-Dagbani Ewe, Ga-Adangme, and Gurma. Despite the variety, there were no serious ethnic dissensions when Ghana became independent. The official language is English. More than one-half of the population is Christian, about one-fifth is Muslim, and a small segment adheres to the traditional indigenous religions.

Like many other African countries, considerable prominence is given to dead ancestors, who are considered ever-present, capable of influencing the course of events for the living and serving as intermediaries between the living and the gods.

Since 1970 Ghana's population has maintained an average annual growth rate above the world average. About two-thirds of Ghanaians are under 30, which ensures that the country's high growth rate will continue for some time. Although low by world standards, life expectancy has improved considerably since 1960 and is among the highest in Western Africa.

Population fluctuations have resulted from emigration. During the Colonial era, descendants of Nigerian Hausas were brought to the Gold Coast, now Ghana, to fight under the British flag in an attempt to destroy one of the last holdouts against British rule in West Africa, the Ashanti Empire. These Hausas contributed to the foundations of the Gold Coast's colonial army.

Emigration between Nigeria and Ghana also became more pronounced during the severe economic depression of the late 1970s and early 1980s.

5. Ghanian Cultures, Customs, and Etiquette

5.1. IMPORTANCE OF UNDERSTANDING AFRICAN CULTURES, CUSTOMS, AND ETIQUETTE

Understanding other African cultures, customs, and etiquette is essential for successful business interactions in Intra-African trade due to the following reasons:

Cultural Sensitivity: Africa is a diverse continent with numerous distinct cultures, languages, and traditions. Each African country has its own unique customs, social norms, and business practices. By understanding and respecting these cultural differences, you demonstrate sensitivity and appreciation for the values and traditions of the countries you engage with. This enhances your ability to establish positive relationships and navigate business transactions effectively.

Relationship Building: Building strong relationships is crucial in African business cultures. Africans prioritize personal connections and trust-building before engaging in business. Understanding the customs, greetings, and social protocols of the specific African cultures you are working with helps establish rapport and trust. It demonstrates your genuine interest and commitment to building long-term partnerships, which is highly valued in many African societies.

Effective Communication: Communication styles and norms vary across African cultures. Verbal and non-verbal cues, indirect communication, and high-context communication may differ from what you are accustomed to. Understanding these nuances allows you to adapt your communication approach, use appropriate language and tone, and interpret messages accurately. This facilitates effective communication, reduces misunderstandings, and fosters productive dialogue and collaboration.

Business Etiquette: Each African country has its own business etiquette and protocols. Understanding these customs helps you navigate formalities, such as greetings, introductions, and appropriate forms of address. Adhering to local business etiquette shows respect and professionalism, leading to smoother business interactions and a positive perception of your commitment to understanding and working within the local cultural context.

Trust and Credibility: Intra-African trade often involves establishing business relationships with unfamiliar partners. Understanding local customs and cultural norms helps build trust and credibility. It shows that you are committed to respecting and adapting to the business practices of the specific African country, which can enhance your reputation and increase the likelihood of successful partnerships.

Cultural Preferences and Market Insights: Understanding African cultures enables you to understand better consumer preferences, market behaviours, and trends within specific African countries. Cultural insight helps shape your products, services, and marketing strategies to align with local preferences, making your offerings more appealing and relevant to the target market. This knowledge enhances your competitive advantage in Intra-African trade.

Overcoming Stereotypes and Biases: Cultural understanding allows you to challenge and overcome stereotypes and biases that may exist about certain African cultures. By actively seeking to understand and appreciate the richness and diversity of African cultures, you can foster a more inclusive and respectful business environment that promotes collaboration and equal opportunities.

In conclusion, understanding other African countries' cultures, customs, and etiquette is vital for a successful business engagement in Intra-African trade. It facilitates effective communication, builds trust, enhances relationships, and enables you to adapt your strategies and practices to align with local expectations. Cultural understanding is key for thriving in Africa's diverse and dynamic business landscape.

5.2. GHANA'S CULTURAL SIGNIFICANCE

Ghana's influential music, literature, and art show the country's cultural significance. The country is known for its highlife music, which combines traditional African rhythms with Western instrumentation and has been influential throughout the continent.

Literature And the Arts In Ghana – Ghana has a rich storytelling tradition. Large audiences still enjoy Ghanaian folktales and epics glorifying past chiefs. Kwaku Ananse, a spider, is a popular figure of Ghanaian folklore. A small body of written literary works is in the country's indigenous languages. Ghana has produced several famous works by renowned writers, including "The Beautyful Ones Are Not Yet Born" by Ayi Kwei Armah, "The Dilemma of a Ghost" by Ama Ata Aidoo, "Faceless" by Amma Darko, "The Ghanaian Sphinx" by Cameron Duodu, and "Ancestral Logic and Caribbean Blues" by Kofi Anyidoho.

Other writers include William Boyd, Akosua Busia, Kofi Awoonor, Kwame Anthony Appiah, Meshack Asare, Joe Coleman de Graft, J. E. Casely Hayford, and Aaron Mike Oquaye.

Dizzee Rascal, Sway, Tinchy Stryder, and Stormzy are some British artists with Ghanaian heritage. AZONTO! Is the dance that has taken the UK by storm. The dance was first invented in Ghana.

Ghana also has a rich tradition of graphic art. For example, Adinkra Symbols are intricate, geometric symbols from the Akan people, traditionally used to convey concepts, values, and proverbs. Kente cloth is a visually striking and intricately woven fabric with great cultural significance in Ghana. Ghanaian artisans excel at wood carving. Stools representing abstract designs or animals are carved out of large logs; these stools become objects of veneration after the deaths of their owners. Sculpting is another craft form of Ghana whereby iron and bronze casting techniques are used to produce ceremonial swords, gold weights, and other products. Ghanaian artisans are active in contemporary illustration and design. They blend traditional influences with modern techniques to create visually captivating artworks, illustrations, and designs for various purposes, including advertising, book covers, and digital media.

Performance Arts in Ghana — Ghanaian music and dance performances were traditionally held in the context of religious or political rites. They were also part of wedding ceremonies, initiation ceremonies, and other social situations. Ghana is often described as a land of festivals, music, and traditional dances. Today, while music and dance continue to serve these purposes, they also symbolize the country's culture. There are three main types of music in Ghana. Ethnic or traditional music is usually played during festivals and funerals. Highlife music blends traditional and imported music. Choral music is performed in concert halls, churches, schools, and colleges. Ghanaian music also widely uses traditional instruments, such as the kora, xylophone, and talking drum. Some of the most famous festivals include the Homowo festival, which celebrates the end of the famine and the start of the harvest season, and the Aboakyir festival, which involves a hunt for a live antelope that is later used in a sacrificial ceremony.

The festival of Homowo is celebrated in the coastal region of Ghana and involves a procession through the streets with people wearing traditional clothes and masks, dancing and chanting. The festival culminates in a feast where dishes such as cornmeal porridge and steamed corn dumplings are shared with friends and family.

The Chale Wote Street Art Festival, held annually in Accra, showcases the work of Ghanaian street artists and muralists, bringing their art to public spaces and engaging with local communities. The festival also features music performances, dance routines, and fashion shows, attracting audiences in Ghana and abroad. During these festivals, people wear traditional attire, perform traditional dances, and enjoy traditional food and drinks. Festivals allow Ghanaians to unite and celebrate their culture and traditions.

Such performances are part of cultural festivals and public occasions also performed in front of tourists. The Ghana Dance Ensemble of the University of Ghana is a cultural institution of global repute. Today, Ghanaian youth, especially those in urban areas, favour contemporary music and dance styles. Highlife and Hiplife are the country's most popular modern music and dance forms,which are usually played in urban nightclubs.

Ghanaian Dancers. Source: *successafrica.info*

Artefacts One thing you will notice with Ghanaians is the vibrancy of colours nationwide. Ghana has some of the best fabrics with bold patterns and millions of styles. Starting with regular regalia to the more sophisticated ceremonial looks, you can see these stunningly beautiful material elements of the culture in Ghana. The country produces not just one but three types of solely African fabrics. These include batik, wax cloth as well as Kente fabric. Even though it uses traditional production methods, the industry is gaining great popularity in modern trends. This places Ghana in a great advantage as cloth making is a big part of Ghana's culture.

The Kente cloth is one of the most recognizable traditional fabrics and is often worn by royalty and during special occasions. Clothing in Ghana also has a symbolic significance, with certain colours and patterns representing different meanings and emotions.

Ghanaian's Kente Cloth. Source: *westafricaadventure.blogspot.com/*

A stool is among Ghana's most valued material components of the culture since it symbolizes power. To be on the stool means to be in power. The importance is derived from the Golden Stool, the royal throne to the Ashanti. In summary, Ghanaian culture is a vibrant and diverse tapestry of customs and traditions that have been passed down through generations.

Traditional medicine

Another traditional practice in Ghanaian culture is the use of traditional medicine. Traditional medicine has been used in Ghana for centuries and is still widely practised today. Herbal medicine is the most common form of traditional medicine in Ghana and is used to treat various ailments. Many Ghanaians believe that traditional medicine is more effective than modern medicine and trust traditional healers to cure their illnesses. Traditional medicine is also seen as a way to connect with the ancestors and the spiritual world. For instance, the moringa plant has been used as a traditional medicine to treat various ailments, such as stomach problems, arthritis, and infections. The plant is also believed to provide energy and boost the immune system.

Herbal Medicine Practice in Ghana. Source: *https://www.modernghana.com/*

Ghanaian culture is rich in beliefs and superstitions

Many Ghanaians believe in the existence of ancestral spirits, and they make offerings to their ancestors to seek their blessings and protection. Some Ghanaians also believe in the power of charms and amulets, which can protect them from harm and bring them good luck. Superstitions are also prevalent in Ghanaian culture, with many people believing in the power of certain numbers, animals, and colours. These beliefs and superstitions reflect Ghanaians' deep connection with their spiritual and cultural heritage.

The number 7 is considered lucky and is often used in traditional rituals and ceremonies. For example, during a traditional wedding ceremony, seven bottles of schnapps are poured to symbolize the union of the bride and groom. Additionally, the owl is seen as a bad omen and is often associated with death in Ghanaian culture. People avoid having an owl in their vicinity or hearing its hoot as they believe it brings misfortune.

Christianity in Ghana

Christianity has a significant presence and influence in Ghana, making it one of the most Christianized countries in Africa. The introduction of Christianity to Ghana dates back to the 15th century when European explorers and missionaries arrived on the coast. Since then, Christianity has grown and become deeply embedded in Ghanaian society.

Ghana's major Christian denominations include Protestantism (Presbyterian, Methodist, Baptist, and Pentecostal churches), Roman Catholicism, and the African Independent Churches (which blend Christian beliefs with traditional African practices).

Christianity plays a central role in the lives of many Ghanaians. Church attendance is high and religious activities are integral to the social fabric. Churches are places of worship and serve as centres for community engagement, education, healthcare, and social services.

Alongside the mainstream denominations, Ghana has a significant presence of Indigenous Churches or African Independent Churches. These churches blend Christian beliefs with African cultural practices and have their unique expressions of worship and spiritual practices.

The Charismatic and Pentecostal movements have experienced remarkable growth in Ghana. These churches emphasize the power of the Holy Spirit, spiritual gifts, and personal experiences of God, and they often feature vibrant worship, faith healing, and prosperity teachings.

Social Impact: Christianity has had a profound impact on Ghanaian society. Churches and Christian organizations actively participate in education, healthcare, community development, and social justice initiatives. They address social issues, promote literacy, provide healthcare facilities, and support vulnerable populations. Christianity in Ghana has been influenced by and has influenced traditional Ghanaian culture. Local languages and cultural practices are incorporated into worship services, music, and religious ceremonies, creating a unique blend of Christianity and indigenous traditions. The religious landscape in Ghana is diverse and contributes to the country's cultural richness and pluralism.

Islam in Ghana

Islam has a notable presence in Ghana and is one of the major religions practised in the country. Islam was first introduced to Ghana through trans-Saharan trade routes as early as the 10th century. It gained significant influence in the northern regions of Ghana, which were part of the larger Sahelian Islamic cultural sphere. According to estimates, Muslims comprise 18% to 20% of the population.

Most Muslims in Ghana are Sunni Muslims. Islam in Ghana is not limited to any particular ethnic group; some Muslims are among the Akan, Mole-Dagbani, Ga-Dangme, and other communities. The largest concentration of Muslims is in the northern regions of Ghana, particularly among the Gonja, Mamprusi, Dagomba, and Hausa communities.

Ghana has a range of Islamic organizations and institutions that promote education, religious guidance, and community development. These include the Office of the National Chief Imam, the Muslim Council of Ghana, and various Islamic schools, madrasas, and universities. Islam in Ghana has integrated with Ghanaian culture, resulting in a unique blend of Islamic practices and local traditions. Muslims in Ghana maintain their religious identity while participating in traditional Ghanaian festivals and cultural events. Islamic organizations and individuals are involved in education, healthcare, social welfare, and philanthropic activities, contributing to the country's overall development. Ghana has a long-standing tradition of religious tolerance and peaceful coexistence between Muslims and Christians. Interfaith dialogue and collaboration between Muslim and Christian communities are encouraged to foster unity and understanding.

Storytelling

Storytelling is a means of passing on knowledge, history, and values from one generation to the next. In Ghana, storytelling and dance are often intertwined, with many dances having a story or message behind them. Ghanaian storytelling is a vibrant art form passed down for centuries. It is a way of preserving the history and culture of the people through the generations. Storytelling in Ghana is not limited to just spoken words but includes music, dance, and drama. The stories are often told through songs and dances that capture the imagination and bring the stories to life. These stories are used to teach moral lessons, provide guidance, and inspire the youth. Dance is also an important aspect of Ghanaian culture and is often used as a form of storytelling. The dances in Ghana are diverse, with each region having its own unique style and rhythm. Some of the most popular dances include Adowa, Kpanlogo, and Agbadza. These dances are often accompanied by live music and are performed during special occasions, such as weddings, funerals, and festivals. Dance is a way for Ghanaians to express themselves and celebrate their culture, and it is a vital part of the Ghanaian identity.

Sports In Ghana – Football (soccer) is Ghana's most popular sport. The country's national football team, known as the Black Stars, has participated in many international football tournaments like the FIFA World Cup and the African Cup of Nations. Football is also played informally throughout the nation. Other popular sporting events in Ghana include tennis, basketball, athletics, rugby, hockey, golf, etc.

Matriarch and Patriarch Influence in Ghanaian Society – Ghana has a cultural framework that includes aspects of both patriarchal and matriarchal influences, although the patriarchal system tends to be more prevalent.

The patriarchal system in Ghana places men in positions of authority and decision-making power within families and communities. Men often hold leadership roles in households, communities, and traditional institutions. They are typically responsible for providing for their families and making important decisions regarding family matters. Ghanaian society also values the extended family structure, where lineage and kinship play a crucial role. The patriarch, often the eldest male in the family, holds significant influence and authority over family affairs. Under the traditional patriarchal system, inheritance and succession are passed down through the male lineage. Sons or other male relatives typically inherit assets, property, and leadership positions.

While Ghanaian culture is predominantly patriarchal, certain ethnic groups and communities exhibit matriarchal influences. In these communities, women usually hold more authority and play central roles in decision-making processes. For instance, the Akan people follow matrilineal descent, where inheritance and family lineage are traced through the mother's side.

Ghanaian women play essential roles in both the private and public spheres. While they may face some cultural and societal limitations, women actively contribute to household management, agriculture, entrepreneurship, and community development. In recent years, progress has been made in advocating for gender equality and empowering women in Ghana.

Marriages in Ghana, especially in rural areas, are still arranged by the parents of the bride and the groom. Polygamous marriages are allowed but depend on the man's financial conditions. The village chiefs often marry many women. A bride's price is paid to the bride's family in exchange for the bride. The primary aim of most marriages is to have children. Women who do not bear children are often divorced by their husbands. Divorce is easy to obtain and is widespread. In urban areas, however, the spread of Western values has influenced marriage customs. Monogamy is preferred, and modern nuclear families are more common.

The basic household unit in Ghana varies in size and composition. The domestic arrangements differ by ethnic group. Patrilocal residence (the bride moves in with the groom's family) and nato-local residence (both bride and groom stay with their respective parents after marriage) are the common domestic arrangements seen in Ghana. Inheritance is matrilineal (for the Akan ethnic group) or patrilineal (for other ethnic groups).

Children are highly valued in society. Mothers are primarily responsible for childcare, with grandparents and relatives participating in this activity. Many initiation ceremonies and puberty rites mark children's transition to adulthood. Both boys and girls are sent to primary and secondary school. High poverty levels and poor infrastructure often prevent children from attending school or lead to high dropout rates. Only a very small percentage of the population can attend a university.

Death and the Afterlife. Death is one of the most important events in society and is marked by most ethnic groups and religions by elaborate and lengthy funeral observances that involve the whole community. When a person dies, the body is buried within a couple of weeks, the family says goodbye, and people bring food and refreshments to the funeral. Funerals are lavish affairs where the deceased's family spends excessive money to feed and entertain many people, indicating how important the person was in life. People were traditionally buried beneath the floors of their houses, but this custom is now practised only by traditional rulers and most people are interred in cemeteries. After death, the soul joins the ancestors in the after-world to be revered and fed by descendants within the family. Eventually, the soul will be reborn within the lineage it belonged to in its past life. People sometimes see a resemblance to a former member in an infant and name it accordingly. They may even apply the relevant kinship term, such as mother or uncle, to the returnee.

Ghana Coffins. Source: *bbc.com*

Work Ethic — Ghanaians' work ethic and working culture are more slow-paced compared to the Western world. People in Ghana are very hard-working, but they believe in striking a balance. A study of the Akan people who do fishing and agriculture shows that they work on all days except those considered holy. They have an array of agrarian and fishing festivals. They use traditional methods to decipher which fish to take and which plants and animals to protect. This method in Ghana's history and culture helps protect the balance and harmony of man and nature. This will prevent overfishing and land destruction to ensure enough productivity to keep the people fed. Harmony and interpersonal relationships are still considered important in the modern workplace. Modern methods continue, however, to be adopted in the different industries that are found in Ghana.

5.3. GHANIAN CUSTOM AND TRADITION

Ghana is a large country with 30 million people. Like most other African nations, Ghana has rich, traditional cultures that differ from one ethnic group to another. So, many of the customs mentioned in this section may vary slightly depending on which ethnic group you are interacting with. The country has six larger groups: the Akan (Ashanti and Fanti), the Ewe, the Ga-Adangbe, the Mole-Dagbani, the Guan and the Gruma.

Along with different ethnic groups and cultures, 52 separate languages and hundreds of dialects are spoken in Ghana. The official language is English since the introduction of the Education Ordinance Act of 1926 by the British, which gave prominence to the proper use of English. It made an English certification a prerequisite for employment in most professions in Ghana.

The people of Ghana are warm and friendly, polite, open and trusting — even with strangers. In Ghanaian society, it is traditional to take life at a relaxed pace and view time as a series of events rather than hours or minutes.

This section uses some feedback from Quoras.com members and qualitative feedback from a sample of non-Ghanians interviewed in the United Kingdom.

Here is a comment from an anonymous Nigerian:

"Ghanaians, in general, are tranquil, laidback, and religious people. They believe in helping their poor family members and see riches not as an end goal but rather as a by-product of God's blessings of one's deeds. As a result, many ordinary Ghanaians do not earnestly seek riches as in Western countries".

In Ghanaian society, people are more important than schedules. Most Ghanaians consider the initial conversation of "let's get to business" with a stranger or somebody they do not know as rude. It is customary for Ghanaians to exchange pleasantries and ask about family before beginning a business transaction. They greet one another, making an extra effort to greet older people. With the men, handshakes almost always accompany greetings.

A handshake is more than a symbol of greeting. This elaborate meeting of palms, thumbs and forefingers begins as a regular handshake; before the two people withdraw their hands, their palms slide together until their middle fingers touch. And then, they turn their hands so that the palms are glimpsed before bringing together their thumb and forefinger for the signature click at the end. A handshake to symbolise friendship and ease can be confusing at first, but it is simple, fun, and a great indicator of showing good spirit and familiarity to a fellow human.

Wiggling the middle fingers in a handshake, followed by a finger snap, is also a profound sign in Ghanaian culture and traditions. This sign means that the two people love one another, not necessarily romantically but more from a social perspective. This is always an icebreaker and a sign of ease and friendship in the culture of Ghana.

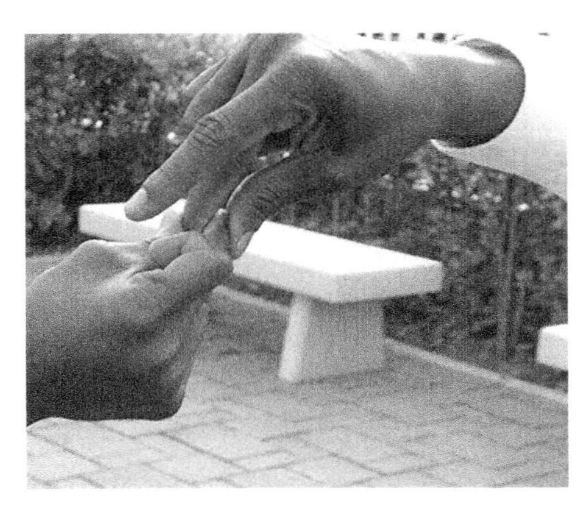

Handshake by snapping the fingers. Source: *ldsghanamtc.blogspot.com*

Similarly, it would help if you never handed anything to a Ghanaian with your left hand unless you want to offend him deeply. Traditionally, before the advent of the toilet and toilet paper, the left hand was used to clean yourself after going to the toilet. In contrast, the right hand was reserved for eating food and interacting with others.

Another important hand gesture is "Tweaka", roughly translated it means 'return to sender' in Ghana, It is used along with a gesture that involves taking a thumb and circling it around one's head before flicking the imaginary circle away and indicating a response when someone has ill will towards you or says something negative.

Relatives and friends often visit each other without warning. Greeting phrases alternate between different ethnic groups.

When greeting, you ask how the other person and his family feel. Visitors greet all the family members of the house.

Ghanaians are very communal. Being greeted with hugs and back pats is not usual when you meet someone for the first time, but it is not uncommon to see people eating a dish from the same plate together. Unlike in many Western countries, Ghanaians like to be in close proximity to each other rather than needing personal space. Also, greeting with a Good Morning, Afternoon, or Evening is customary when you enter a room.

Family provides a very strong bond in Ghana and is the primary source of identity, loyalty, and responsibility. Family obligations take precedence over everything else in life, and individuals achieve recognition and social standing through their extended family.

As mentioned earlier, a fascinating cultural variation among the Akan, or Ashanti and Fanti people, is that affiliation within the clan is derived through women. Mothers have a higher status since, from their point of view, people get their blood from their mothers.

Ghanaians need to maintain dignity, honour, and a good reputation. The entire family shares any loss of honour, making the culture collective. To protect this sense of face, there is a need to maintain a sense of harmony; people will always act with decorum to ensure they do not cause embarrassment.

You are obliged to invite others to eat with you. (They will almost always say "Thank you", — which means "No, thank you") and then continue to eat your meal. Polite behaviour is important. For example, if you yawn or use a toothpick, you must hold your mouth. Staring or pointing at someone in front of others is also inappropriate.

Ghanaian society is hierarchical. People are respected because of their age, experience, wealth and/or position. Older people are viewed as wise and are granted respect. You must address Ghanaians by their academic, professional, or honorific title and surname. As a sign of respect, males over the age of 30 may be addressed as "pah-pah", while women of the same age may be called "mah-mee". People over the age of 50 may be referred to as "nah-nah". One can always see preferential treatment for the eldest member of a group. However, with respect comes responsibility, and people expect the most senior person to make decisions in the group's best interest.

Ghanaians enjoy entertaining in their homes, and any invitation should be regarded as a sign of friendship. Ghanaians place a lot of emphasis on how people dress. You may need to remove your shoes when entering a Muslim home.

There are also differences between the urban and rural populations in dress and eating habits, with the urban dwellers being distinctly more Westernized and sophisticated. Ghana possesses a rich indigenous cuisine. Reflecting the country's agricultural wealth and varied historical connections, it includes fufu (starchy foods—such as cassava, yams, or plantains—that are boiled, pounded, and rolled into balls), kenke (fermented cornmeal wrapped in plantain leaves or corn husks), groundnut (peanut) soup, palm nut soup, fish, and snails.

Ghanaians place a high value on dignity and proper social conduct and individual conduct is seen as impacting an entire family, social group, and community. Therefore, everyone is expected to be respectful, dignified, and observant in nearly every aspect of life.

AP (Kenyan): "People *from West Africa, especially the Nigerians and Ghanaians, do look alike. Their demeanour is the easiest way to differentiate Ghanaians from Nigerians. While Ghanaians are generally more tranquil and laid back, Nigerians are generally loud, aggressive, and arrogant and will do anything to make it in life".*

Ghanaians are also perceived as indirect communicators who avoid relaying any information that could cause issues. This includes delivering bad news, rejecting an invitation, refusing a request, or taking a different point of view. Generally, Ghanaians would want to protect their face and maintain harmonious relationships throughout society. Silence is often a typical means of communication for Ghanaians. Suppose A Ghanaian is uncomfortable with a question or does not think the asker will appreciate his different opinion. In that case, he will say nothing rather than make the other person uncomfortable. This sometimes comes across as a lack of confidence, and other Africans frown on this as h they feel you can never be sure what a Ghanaian is thinking about an issue. Ghanaians will sometimes not say what they mean in a meeting and may later do something else.

Generally, Ghanaians tend to be non-confrontational and highly considerate of others during communication. Therefore, they generally resist saying things that could be perceived as embarrassing for others. It is common for Ghanaians to understate their opinion to remain polite and harmonious. For example, it may not always be immediately evident when they have been offended. Therefore, one often has to rely on reading non-verbal cues to draw further meaning.

Refusals: Ghanaians can be quite hesitant to give direct refusals, especially when asked to perform a favour by a friend. This can mean they agree to do something they do not want to or cannot do to avoid sounding rude. If you receive a final answer that is unsettled (e.g. "maybe", "let's wait and see" or "let me think about that"), it is generally a good indicator that they mean "no".

Education is highly valued in Ghanaian culture. Despite challenges such as poverty and lack of resources, Ghanaians prioritise education and see it as a key to success and upward mobility. Many parents make great sacrifices to ensure their children receive a good education. Ghana has made significant strides in improving access to education in recent years. Ghanaians hold education in high regard because it has proven to be the country's consistent leveller and equalizer. Many have risen from the gutters to prestigious statuses due to the education they acquired, so people prioritize education even when they migrate to other countries. A 2015 report by the Migration Policy Institute noted that about 18% of Ghanaian diaspora members in the U.S. aged 25 and over had a bachelor's degree as their highest credential, and about 12% of Ghanaian diaspora members had an advanced degree, compared to about 11% of the overall U.S. population. According to the renowned US-based plastic surgeon Dr Michael Obeng, there are more Ghanaian physicians in New York City than in Ghana.

Ghanaian is considered a collectivist society; individuals pursuing success are committed to the well-being, pride, and prosperity of the family or tribe. As a result, parents push their children and drive them to achieve, and the children are imbued with this cultural belief.

The meaning of the word Charlie or Charley in Ghana

Charlie pronounced "Charley", has two roots, one from colonial times and another from the Ga word 'Charle-wote'.

When Gold Coast (Ghana) was under British imperial rule, the British lords had many names, obviously, but for some reason, the ones that stood out in Ghana were Charlie and Jack. The names became so popular amongst the Gold Coasters (Ghanaians) that they began to refer to strangers as Charlie/Jack, much like Americans use "dude". Over time, Charlie became "Charley" though Jack remained Jack. The word "Charlie" means friend.

"Charle" was derived from the Ga word 'Charle-wote', which means "my friend let's go". Charle-wote is a name given to a type of rock-hard bathroom slippers. The Ga people are known for their hurriedness in doing stuff, and the Ghanaian youths also like roaming around (they struggle to sit idle in a place for a long time). Therefore, these slippers (Charle wote) are very fast and easy to wear, especially when escaping punishment or house chores, symbolising the wandering youths. Everyone is Charle in Ghana.

Pidgin English is spoken in Ghana and anglophone West and Central African countries. It first came about in the 17th and 18th centuries when the Europeans colonized Africa. It began as a combination of English vocabulary and the different languages spoken by the ethnic groups the British traded with at the time. Pidgin is an informal language (developed over time by interacting with the various local and English languages, with few foreign imports) spoken in Ghana and many other African countries, especially Nigeria.

Ghanaian Pidgin is a mixture of English and local dialects, like Akan and Ga. It is an essential language for conducting business in the markets and makes commuting around the country relatively easy as it is the language for bargaining in the markets and with drivers. Ghanaian Pidgin, like other West African Pidgin, is very adaptive. New words emerge and catch on rather quickly than the frequency of words added to the dictionary.

Standard English otherwise dominates in most formal settings, but Ghanaian Pidgin English, also known as Kru English or Kroo Brofo in Akan, has two sub-varieties. There is the non-institutionalized or uneducated pidgin, usually spoken or associated with illiterates, and the institutionalized or educated one, spoken in Senior high schools and Universities.

Ghanaian Timekeeping – Ghanaian time is the perceived cultural tendency of Ghanaians toward a more relaxed attitude to time. This usually expresses in Ghanaians' tardiness for appointments, meetings and events. This also includes the more leisurely, relaxed, and less rigorously scheduled lifestyle found in many African countries, as opposed to the more clock-bound pace of daily life in Western countries.

However, Ghanaian's lax attitude towards time reflects a different approach to managing tasks, events, and interactions. For example, a Ghanaian tends to have more "emotional time consciousness", which contrasts with Western "mechanical time consciousness".

The reality is that this lax attitude to time was typical in all agricultural societies worldwide before the middle of the eighteenth century – the beginning of the Industrial Revolution. Before this period, in most cultures, the natural rhythms of the days and the seasons were sufficient for the farmer, and all times were local.

From the late seventeenth century, the accuracy of the time mechanisms gradually improved because coordination was essential for industries to bring supplies of raw materials together, organise workers, and distribute their output. Factories demanded all the workers arrive simultaneously to run the machines and start production. Workers were also made to work per hour to improve their productivity and deliver orders on time.

Ghanaian time has become a key topic of self-criticism. Some believe that one of the main reasons for the continuing underdevelopment of Ghana is the carefree attitude towards time and the need for punctuality in all aspects of life.

Ghanaian Cuisine — A standard meal in Ghana features a staple carbohydrate dish served with sauces, soups, or stews. Tomatoes are extensively added to the soups and stews, which thus have a red or orange colour. The diet includes cassava and plantain in northern Ghana and millet and sorghum in southern Ghana. Sweet potatoes, maize, and beans are also used in various dishes. Rice and wheat have been introduced in the country recently and are growing in importance as staples of the diet. Beef, lamb, goat, pork, chicken, smoked turkey, dried snails, fried fish, seafood, etc., are usually added to the soups and stews of Ghanaian cuisine. Various spices are added, such as thyme, ginger, peppers, garlic, bay leaf, nutmeg, etc. Bread of different types, like tea bread, brown bread, butter bread, oat bread, rye bread, etc., are consumed for breakfast. Most widely consumed Ghanaian alcoholic beverages included drinks made from fermented maize, palm wine, a local beer made from fermented millet called pitoo, etc. Popular non-alcoholic beverages include cocoa drinks, yogurt, ice cream, soy milk, soft drinks, etc.

The Jollof Wars — The rivalry between Nigerian and Ghanaian styles of Jollof is a (mostly light-hearted) debate among the West African diaspora. Jollof is a piquant seasoned rice dish that's a medley of rice, tomatoes, and spices. It is generally eaten as a main dish in most West African countries and a staple at parties and family gatherings. At its base, it is stewed rice with tomatoes, onions, vegetable or olive oil, habanero (or scotch bonnet) pepper, tomato puree (or tin tomatoes), stock cubes, thyme, curry powder, ginger, and garlic. Spices, ingredients, and cooking methods vary slightly between households, but the basic elements of rice, tomatoes, and onions remain the same. However, jollof is more than its ingredients. The cooking process is intricate, the order in which you add the ingredients matters, and the person making it matters the most.

Jollof's origins can be traced to Senegal's ancient Wolof empire and medieval state in the 1300s, where it first surfaced as a dish called thiéboudienne. As the Wolof empire grew and dispersed along the West African coast and region, so did the recipe, which was named after one of the biggest Wolof states, Jolof. The rising popularity of rice (introduced into the region from Asia but now grown locally) led to the spread and adaptation of the recipe.

Jollof rice in Nigeria and Ghana is ubiquitous yet highly sought after. You cannot do a party in Nigeria or Ghana without a jollof rice. Cooking methods vary between Nigerian and Ghanaian Jollof, but the main difference is the type of rice used. In making Jollof, Nigerians use long-grain rice, which is sturdier and provides good flavour absorption, while Ghanaians use the more-aromatic basmati rice, which itself adds an extra flavour to the dish

Jollof with chicken. Source *www.eater.com*

5.4. GHANA AND NIGERIA'S RELATIONSHIP

The Ghana-Nigeria rivalry has existed for as long as both countries have existed. Though the two countries do not share borders, they are separated by Togo and Benin and always behave as if they were neighbours. It has something to do with the two countries being English-speaking and British colonies amid francophone countries.

Ghana and Nigeria are two of the largest and most influential countries in West Africa. As neighbouring nations with similar histories and cultures, they have had a complex and sometimes tense relationship.

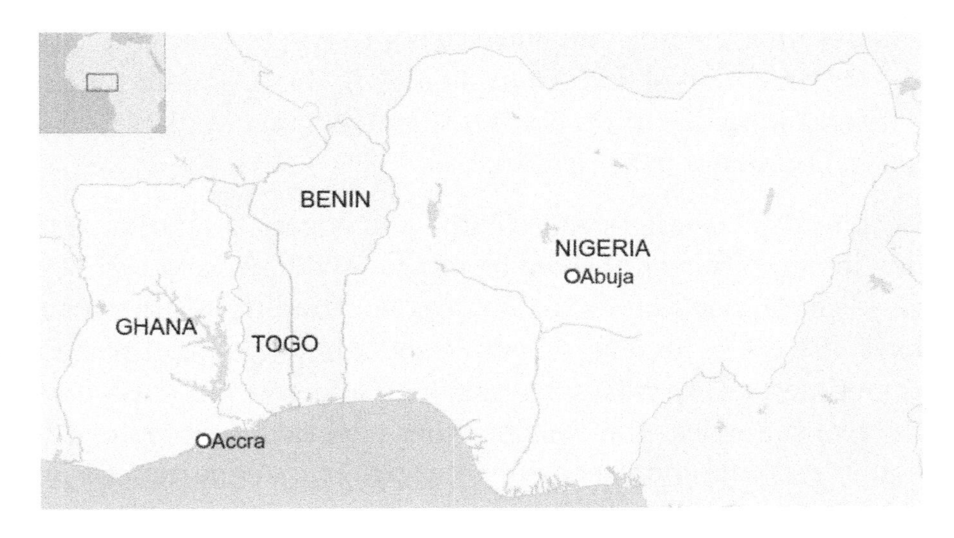

Map of Ghana and Nigeria. Source *bbc.com*

Ghana and Nigeria both have rich histories, with powerful empires that thrived before European colonization. Ghana was home to the Ashanti Empire, which controlled a large part of West Africa, while Nigeria was home to several powerful empires, including the Hausa-Fulani, Yoruba, and Kanem-Bornu empires. These empires traded with each other and shared cultural and religious practices.

During the colonial era, Ghana and Nigeria were under British rule, with Nigeria being a much larger and more complex colony. The two countries did not have a direct relationship during this time, as other British colonies separated them. However, both countries were heavily influenced by British culture and institutions.

After gaining independence in the 1950s and 1960s, Ghana and Nigeria became leaders in the pan-African movement and played important roles in the decolonization of the continent. Ghana's first president, Kwame Nkrumah, was a leading advocate for African unity and played a key role in the formation of the Organization of African Unity (OAU), the precursor to the African Union. Nigeria's first president, Nnamdi Azikiwe, was also a prominent pan-Africanist.

Despite these shared goals, Ghana and Nigeria's relationship has sometimes been marked by tension. While Ghana and Nigeria share many cultural practices and traditions, they also have distinct languages, religions, and ethnic groups. This has sometimes led to misunderstandings and tensions between the two countries. The two countries have kept up the neighbourly rivalries and friendships through mass deportations in the 1980s and 1990s.

In the 1950s, many Nigerians began moving to Ghana after Ghana became the first independent country in the region in 1957. The Progress Party government's Aliens Compliance Order of November 1969 ordered all undocumented residents to leave Ghana. While this law applied to citizens of several West African countries, such as Togolese, Burkinabes, and Ivorians, Nigerians, mostly ethnic Yorubas from the southwestern states of Nigeria, formed most of the foreign population in Ghana. Some had lived in Ghana for decades and were in their second and third generations. It felt like the exercise aimed at Nigerians and their unpleasant journeys home.

In the 1970s, millions of Ghanaian migrants were attracted to Nigeria because of the 1970s oil boom. As Nigeria became rich, Ghana's economy collapsed; from around 1974, the departure to Nigeria was on. Most Ghanaians that went to Nigeria worked as nannies, maidservants, cooks, and gardeners; some worked as school teachers.

As someone growing up in Nigeria's cities in the 1980s, you would have had a Ghanaian nanny or maidservant, a Ghanaian cook or gardener, and you would have been taught by a Ghanaian teacher at school or as a private tutor.

Then in 1983, the economy of Nigeria began to weaken. President Shagari of Nigeria's order, in alleged response to the religious disturbances that had engulfed parts of the country in 1980 (known as the Kano Riots), announced the expulsion of all undocumented residents . Since Ghanaians constituted most of these people, it felt like this was aimed at Ghanaians.

During the 1980s expulsion of Ghanaians, the primary route to Ghana was westwards, passing through Benin and Togo.

"**Ghana Must Go" bag** – A type of cheap matted woven nylon-zipped tote bag used by the migrants to move their belongings got the name "Ghana Must Go" during the migration.

Ghana must Go bag. Source: *pulse.ng*

The expulsion of more than one million Ghanaian nationals, mostly young people without employable skills, from Nigeria in 1983 delivered a further shock to the economy when they returned to Ghana. But this immigration failed to cause major socio-political upheavals, owing largely to the impressive absorptive capacity of Ghana's indigenous social systems.

Over the years, Ghanaians and Nigerian leaders have returned to building a relationship because they realised that they couldn't do much without each other.

The West African regional organisation, Ecowas, had come into being in 1975, and the two major English-speaking countries needed each other to make things work.

The current tensions between the two countries are being blamed on bilateral trade differences. A Ghanaian law restricts foreigners from retail trade — and Ghanaian traders do not want Nigerian traders in the markets.

According to Ghana's law, foreigners in Ghana can't run small retail shops, but they can own wholesale firms or other businesses in which around $1m (£782,000) has been invested. The law protects smaller local traders and those running small businesses like barbers or beauty salons but is not always enforced. Market traders have sometimes taken the law into their own hands, which prompted the authorities to audit retail shops in August and close some Nigerian-run stalls. Foreigners married to a Ghanaian are exempt from the laws — as are those in a business partnership with a Ghanaian.

Nigerians are especially visible in the retail trade sector in Ghana.

MA (Ghanian) — *"I am a Ghanaian, and I see Nigerians as hardworking and entrepreneurial. They make 'survival struggles' better as hustlers in Ghana than most Ghanaians."*

This perception has been around for a while.

According to a 50-year-old **Ghanaian**, "*When I was a child, there was a Nigerian woman shopkeeper in almost every town and village in Ghana. We called them "Mami Alata". This meant "a woman that sold everything, and you could wake her up in the middle of the night to buy three sugar cubes"*.

I A (Ghanian) — *Nigerians have more of an eye for business than Ghanaians, making their country a better destination for business and investment partners. But Ghanaians are friendlier. Foreigners have the 'luxury' of enjoying our public transport. Ghana has a better and more effective education system than Nigeria. About 90% of international students at Ghanaian universities are Nigerians."*

KK (Ghanaian) — "*We see Nigerians as too loud, abrasive, and chaotic, and we believe they think they can outsmart everybody, especially Ghanaians. And they think we Ghanaians are too submissive, not very smart, consistently punching above our weight, and nothing upsets them more than Ghana defeating Nigeria. Nothing upsets Nigerians more than Ghana defeating Nigeria in anything, especially football*".

But Nigerians also perceive Ghanaians differently.

AA (Nigerian) — "*Ghanaians don't like to be bothered. They like their social life more than their business. I once went to a grocery shop on my street to buy some food items, and it was just around 5 pm. The attendant told me he was closed even though I was looking at what I wanted to buy, but I couldn't have it. Even with me holding my money, he kept repeating, I've closed chale, I've closed for the day, as a Nigerian that was strange to me, close at 5 pm?*

In Nigeria, you don't close shop until customer traffic ends. You close when there are no more customers.......... but this man said he was closed at 5 pm though the shop was still open, and he didn't leave the shop until night. Customers came, and he would not sell to them, still telling them he was closed for the day. Later, I learnt from someone that Ghanaians also don't like to be bothered. You cannot force them to sell if they do not want to."

AK (Nigerian) — *"I went to a street shop (Kiosk) and met a woman. She had two types of groundnuts: the seed coat (groundnut A) and the one without the seed coat (groundnut B). I needed 10 Ghc ($2)-worth of groundnut B while she only had about 2 Ghc ($0.42) worth of it. However, she has groundnut. I expected her to remove quickly (won't take more than a minute) the seed-coat from groundnut A and sell it to me. This woman gave me back my balance (8Ghc/$1.59) and told me that Groundnut B was finished. This means she has lost this money that could have been hers. I asked her if she couldn't quickly process the other one (groundnut A) so I could buy it. She told me that she is busy. The only 'being busy' I could see was the television before her. This won't happen in Nigeria because the seller will do everything possible to make an effort a sale."*

But many appreciate the similarities between these two countries

AF (Ghanaian) — "*Even though Ghana and Nigeria are both in West Africa, you will have different experiences living there. The easiest way to explain this is to use US and Canada as examples, with Nigerian being the US and Ghana being Canada."*

SB (Ghanaian) — "*Nigeria and Ghana are pretty similar. Although Ghanaians are more cool-headed than Nigerians, Nigeria is a much bigger and more dynamic country. People are friendly in both countries. Ghana is not as muti-ethnic and muti-cultural as Nigeria. Tribalism isn't so much of an issue in Ghana, unlike Nigeria, where every tribe claims to be superior. Other than that, they are pretty similar people with a shared cultural history and history of interaction.*

SO (Nigerian) – *"Ghanaians are very friendly, females are usually much more friendly than males. But note that the males used to be your good friends but started to hate you once the Nigerians started to earn some good money from their country.".*

AY (Nigerians) – *Ghana is not too different from Nigeria, just an 'excerpt'. The people of Ghana are calm and welcoming.*

- *They express their country well with their colours, reflecting almost everything.*
- *The way they pronounce some English words is different from us Nigerians.*
- *They like to challenge and show they are better than Nigerians. For instance, the* ***Jollof rice war*** *that none of the countries has won.*
- *I used to think they were all dark in complexion, but I met some light-skinned Ghanaians on coming here.*
- *Their pidgin is different from ours, and Ghanaian pidgin is like broken Nigerian pidgin.*
- *They are intelligent but not as streetwise as Nigerians.*
- *Ghanaians are way less aggressive than Nigerians and seem laid-back in their business approach. We Nigerians are ready to grab the bull by the balls when shove comes to push.*

How is life in Ghana compared to Nigeria?

KC (Nigerian) – *"Ghanians have a steady water supply, which we all know is one of the human physiological needs. There is always 24hrs of the power supply! Uninterrupted! The bill is there for you to pay, and not in Nigeria. Even after you have paid your NEPA bills, they will still interrupt the power anyhow. There is* *enough security at their different borders. At least for this one, you are sure of a well-secured environment. Means of transportation is also well defined! The roads were smooth and different sizes of vehicles had their own route to ply on...But in all these, the cost of living in Ghana is quite expensive to that of Nigeria".*

JYF (Ghanian) — _ *"Everything depends on which angle you're looking at it. If you are a Nigerian used to the hustle and bustle of Lagos, you'd see Ghana as calmer and more orderly than Nigeria. And you'd find Ghana more liveable compared to Nigeria. This is because there is virtually 24/7 electricity and the security is superb. Apart from being safer than most in Nigeria, respecting the rule of law is the best in West Africa. The traffic situation in Ghana is better than in Nigeria, and foreigners are much safer than they would have been if there were in Nigeria. Foreigners can take public transport if they are white. This would be nearly impossible in Nigeria."*

PO (Nigerian) — *"Housing is expensive in Ghana; landlords will charge a Nigerian at least two years or more upfront, whereas other foreigners even pay monthly or every six months. I still don't know why? A Ghanaian told me it's because all Nigerians are rich people, and that's how they perceive them in Ghana".*

AA (Nigeria) — *"In Ghana, the education system is different than in Nigeria. What's considered an apprenticeship in Nigeria is considered a school in Ghana. For instance, a Ghanaian learning a fashion design trade will tell you she's in school... Will wear a uniform and will graduate like a normal secondary school student. In Ghana, you can do your Junior Secondary school first and then come back after some years, "let us say after three years", to start your Senior Secondary School. Whereas in Nigeria, that's very rare. You finish Junior School and then start Senior school immediately; you finish your six years once and for all.*

BA (Nigerian) – "*I'm Nigerian, schooling in Ghana. Obviously, their education system is better and more stable than in Nigeria. My first month in Ghana was bittersweet. It was nice to have electricity most of the time. However, it got worse at a point. Having the freedom to move around at 2 in the morning without being scared of robbers or kidnappers is nice. Their food is manageable; they stir-fry everything and the food is expensive. Their food is too fatty, Gobe, Waakye, and Banku. When I return to Nigeria, I appreciate home more, though it is smelly, with the radio blaring and the hustle and bustle in bus stops, but nothing compares. Don't forget that development in Ghana only extends to Accra, Kumasi being the second best. The rest is a village from my point of view.*"

PT (Nigerian) – "*Ghana believes in its people, but Nigeria believes in its name. Ghana makes life easier for its citizens compared to Nigeria. You have to strive for yourself.*

Nigeria has better buildings, structures, and road networks, but Ghana is doing better in power generation (electricity). Ghana is more secure and peaceful due to its low population, and Nigeria, on the other hand, is like a battlefield due to its larger population. Nigeria is doing better in daytime social life, while Ghanaians are doing better at night. Life as a Nigerian is more than a Ghanaian, and the two countries have much in common".

(Nigerian) – "*In my first month in Ghana, I was on a bus when I threw out a sachet of water I had just drank. The conductor or "mate" as they are popularly called in Ghana, sternly warned me against doing that next time. He said I should have put it in the trash on the bus, and it would have been properly disposed of at the end of the day. This experience influenced my impression of Ghana and Ghanaians in general. Most Nigerians see Ghanaians as more morally upright and peaceful. We love our Ghanaian brothers and sisters.*"

AY (Nigerian) – *"I think both countries hold each other with great admiration and healthy sibling rivalry. As a diaspora, I look out for Ghanaians to befriend everywhere I go. Why? They are cool, social, educated, stylish, friendly, and equally outgoing like Nigerians. We share similar colonial and cultural histories. And apart from their slightly darker hue and screechy accent, you can hardly tell Nigerians and Ghanaians apart.*

What's there not to fancy about Ghanaians? Great music, dance steps, delicious food, great football, and stable polity. And what's more, their capital, Accra, though not as sparkling new as Abuja nor as boisterous and commercially sophisticated as Lagos, is a calm, orderly and lively city."

KA (Nigerian) – *"In 2005, I visited Ghana on vacation for a couple of days; the flight was about 60 minutes from Lagos, and it felt like visiting Abuja from Lagos. On arrival, one of the immigration guys had this big grin that I interpreted to be "You know how it is in Naija now, drop something". I ignored him.*

It was a memorable visit; while I waited for my friend Francois to pick me up at a pub, they played Nigerian hits, including Nigeria's Jajagaja by Eedris Abdulkareem, quite a hit then. It turned out that Nigerian hits were also considered to be hits in Ghana."

AJ (Nigerian) – *"I am a Nigerian living in Ghana. Ghana is my second home. Here in Ghana, I do business and move around freely without worrying about any robbery or kidnapping. In Nigeria, a whole area within a community used to contribute money to pay off armed robbers to avoid being attacked at night. I've never heard that in Ghana. Why shouldn't I feel comfortable here?*

After schooling in Zenith, my friends and I, who are also Nigerians, decided to stay in Ghana and not go back to Nigeria because life is good and enjoyable here."

GH (British) — *"During 40 years working at a major UK international airport with arrivals from Lagos and Accra, I encountered far more Ghanaian nationals than Nigerians who spoke no English at all (or, at least, claimed not to). Most of these seemed to be Twi speakers, and we had a supply of Twi-speaking interpreters on call for such eventualities. I only ever met one Nigerian passport-holder who spoke no English — and he turned out to be a Togolese or Beninois national (I forget exactly which) with a forged passport."*

5.5. NIGERIA'S DYING FACTORIES AND EXODUS TO GHANA

Hundreds of Nigerian manufacturing companies have folded up over the years, the surviving ones are grasping for breath, and some plan to relocate to Ghana, a country recently described as 'the new world's factory'.

A World Bank Enterprise survey reported 322 private firms closed down in Nigeria between 2009 and 2014 due to stifling business regulations, corruption, and the political environment. The shortlist includes Berec Batteries; Exide Batteries; Okin Biscuits; Osogbo Steel Rolling Mills; Nigeria Sugar Company; Bacita; Tate and Lyle Sugar Company; Matches Manufacturing Company, Ilorin; Nigeria Paper Mill Limited located in Jebba, Kwara State; Nigerian Newsprint Manufacturing Company Limited, Oku-Iboku, Akwa Ibom State; and the Nigerian National Paper Manufacturing Company Limited in Ogun State.

Others include Nigeria's six automobile assembly plants, namely Peugeot Automobile Nigeria Limited, Kaduna, set up in 1975; Volkswagen of Nigeria Limited, Lagos, established in 1978; Anambra Motor Manufacturing Limited, Emene, Enugu, set up in 1980; Steyr Nigeria Limited Bauchi; National Truck

Manufacturers, Kano; Fiat Production; and Leyland Nigeria Limited Ibadan.

The most troubled industrial sector, perhaps, is Nigeria's textile industry. A liberalisation policy that opened Nigerian borders to cheaper textiles from China and smuggled foreign textiles killed the once vibrant and thriving textile industry.

Nigeria's misfortunes have turned to Ghana's gain thanks to the Economic Commission of West African States' free trade treaty. Some local businesses have relocated to Ghana, a neighbouring country with stable electricity and a more business-friendly environment. In 2006, two of Nigeria's leading tyre manufacturers, Michelin and Dunlop, relocated their factories to Ghana, citing the epileptic energy supply in Nigeria as the chief reason.

Ghana is replacing Nigeria as West Africa's aviation hub for major international airlines, which used to have their regional operational headquarters in Lagos but have moved to Accra, Ghana. These airlines refuel in and route their journeys to Ghana after picking up passengers in Nigeria. Reasons for their relocation are the high cost and scarcity of aviation fuel, poor navigational and landing aids, general scarcity, obsolete infrastructure, and the poor value of the naira. Recently, some Nigeria-bound flights were diverted to Ghana, causing a national embarrassment.

There are speculations that multinationals, such as Cadbury Nigeria Plc, Paterson Zochonis (PZ), Unilever, and Guinness Plc, are considering the feasibility and viability of moving their factories to Ghana, a country fast overtaking Nigeria as West Africa's leading business hub. The author's recent visit to Ghana revealed a large influx of foreign tourists and immigrants.

If Ghana manages its fortunes well, it may be on its way to becoming the Dubai of West Africa.

Reasons for falling business and divesture of many companies from Nigeria are well-known and include unstable energy supply, insecurity, kidnappings, insurgency, the congestion of ports, a poor railway infrastructure, the import dependency of most manufacturing companies, the high cost of forex, multiple tax regimes, a poor social infrastructure, heavy traffic around industrial estates, traffic gridlock to Nigeria's major ports of Apapa and Tin Can Island, and the sharp and shady practices of competitors who import finished products.

5.6. LESSONS FROM GHANAIANS ABOUT MANAGING PANDEMICS

As of the end of 2021, Ghana accounted for only 1,462 deaths reported globally despite containing 30 million people. Ghana's comparatively low mortality rate from COVID-19 significantly defies early predictions of a mass COVID-19 catastrophe and shows that Ghana has salient lessons to teach the rest of the world.

At the beginning of the COVID-19 pandemic, Ghana, like other African countries, had many predictions of doom and gloom. Experts feared that the country's weak healthcare systems, high poverty rates, and lack of clean water and sanitation would make it particularly vulnerable to the virus. These predictions led to concerns that Ghana could face a devastating outbreak, with thousands of deaths on the street and widespread economic devastation.

However, as the pandemic progressed, it became clear that these dire predictions did not come to fruition. Despite initial fears, the number of confirmed COVID-19 cases and deaths in Ghana has been relatively low compared to other regions.

This book believes that the factors that helped Ghana experience low morbidity and mortality from COVID-19 are essential and valuable global public health lessons.

Early Government Measures and Messaging: Ghanaian governments enacted an early response measure to the pandemic on 5 February 2020, even before a single case was reported in the country. On 22 April 2020, the World Health Organization (WHO) highlighted examples of how African countries were leading the global response. By 15 April 2020, Ghana had at least five 'stringent public health and social measures' to prepare for the emerging pandemic. Early border closures and lockdowns were enforced, resulting in less international connectivity to prevent viral importation from incoming flights. All these had an important early impact on slowing the spread.

Ghanian governments were able to implement this quickly because destructive epidemics are not a new phenomenon in Ghana as the country constantly deals with abundant infectious diseases (e.g., malaria, yellow fever, tuberculosis, Ebola, and polio). Consequently, the government has developed effective public health programs with messaging to unify the community and highlight the need for preventative action among individuals. Unlike the governmental mistrust in the Western world, Ghana's population is better prepared to adhere to the government's public health recommendations.

Population Distribution and Structure of Social Networks: It is well documented that the COVID-19 burden is heavily skewed towards older populations. Ghana is fortunate because the country has the youngest population, with a median age of 20. In addition, culturally, most old Ghanaians live independently and are spread throughout their communities. Few older Ghanaian people live together in nursing homes, unlike in the US or the UK, and it is in elderly nursing homes where more than half of deaths occur.

More than half of Ghana still lives in rural areas, usually in well-spaced, well-ventilated houses with natural vegetation. Since infected persons usually transmit the virus through coughing, sneezing, talking, singing, and breathing, studies show that coronavirus transmission is concentrated in indoor settings up to 19 times more than outdoors. As a result, environments in rural areas well-ventilated with outside air significantly reduce the chance of viral transmission compared to tightly enclosed indoor spaces in developed countries, especially during the cold winter. In contrast, most of Ghana's deaths happen to the social and political elites that live and work in airconditioned closed spaces in the cities. Furthermore, people that live in rural areas primarily tend to be farmers, and this profession favours dawn-to-dusk outdoor lifestyles. Prolonged, year-round outdoor living with direct exposure to sun and UV light in Ghana also reduces transmission, with the additional benefit of vitamin D produced by the sun.

Trained Immunity: The phenomenon of trained immunity may have reduced the COVID-19 statistics in Ghana. For example, live vaccines activate innate immune systems, protecting against future infections from other pathogens. Recent data suggest that countries like Ghana, where BCG vaccinations are mandatory, have lower COVID-19 disease burden.

The "Hygiene Hypothesis" stipulates that Ghana's general poor hygiene may have helped reduce COVID-19 infection. Studies show that some environments offer their populations advantages against certain forms of infection and disease due to chronic exposure to a multi-microbial and dirty environment. Over time, this compels their body to produce protective immune effects when encountering new pathogens. While cleanliness is often preferred and next to Godliness, there has been some concern regarding countries that are overly clean and regularly use ultra-hygienic practices, exemplified by the overuse of hand sanitiser and other disinfection practices. Ghana is one of the most vulnerable countries to infectious disease epidemics. As a result, Ghana's population carries the heaviest burden of such diseases. For example, infections by malaria alone may have helped strengthen Ghana's human immune system further and make its body defiant to new diseases, thereby conferring an immune advantage to the populace.

Ghana's use of traditional medicine during COVID – Traditional medicine comprises of unscientific knowledge systems that developed over generations within various societies before the era of Western medicine. Many traditional medicine practitioners in Africa have gained knowledge of medicinal plants and their effects on the human body. Such knowledge is passed on orally from father to son through generations. The components of traditional medicine encompass herbal medicine, therapeutic fasting and dieting, and more. The practitioners include herbalists, diviners, and midwives.

The natural medicine for primary care and its effectiveness in Ghana during the pandemic triggered a World Health Organisation (WHO-AFRO) expert panel in September 2020 to endorse a protocol for the clinical investigation of herbal medicine for COVID-19.

Modern pharmaceuticals and medical procedures have remained unaffordable and inaccessible to many Ghanaians due to their relatively high cost. Traditional medicine has become the natural alternative for many Ghanaians, as it is affordable and accessible to ordinary citizens in rural and urban areas. The remedies made from indigenous plants play a crucial role in the health of millions of Africans. One estimate puts the number of Africans routinely using traditional medicine services as their first choice before Western medicine to be as high as 85% in Sub-Saharan Africa.

Genetics: Some genetic and immunological factors could have played a role in shielding Ghanaians from the brunt of the pandemic. Studies have shown that African populations have an exceptionally high proportion of O-positivity, at nearly 50%, higher than White and Asian populations. This increased O prevalence may have conferred a greater protective effect in Ghanaian populations compared with other groups with less O prevalence.

In conclusion, the relatively low severity and death due to COVID-19 in Ghana presents somewhat of a paradox. While the media says very little about it, it is a great success that Ghana and other African countries should be proud of and talk about.

6. The Future of Ghana's Cocoa Trade on the World Market

Ghana is internationally known for its cocoa production and trade. As a second-leading world cocoa producer, it registered an annual minimum cocoa bean output of 1.1 million metric tons in 2020/2021.

The Ghana Cocoa Board (COCOBOD), the government institution responsible for regulating cocoa buying prices, identified some threats to cocoa production in Ghana. For decades, cocoa has remained the backbone of Ghana's economy, providing a source of livelihood to about 800,000 small-scale cocoa farmers who make up 60% of the country's agricultural base. However, despite their contribution to Ghana's development, many cocoa-farming families live in abject poverty — mainly due to low cocoa prices on the international market. Over the years, Ghana has earned less than the value of raw cocoa supplied to the world market. Statistics show that cocoa farmers earn a per capita daily income of approximately US$0.40 — $0.45 from cocoa. This amounts to an annual net income of US$983.12 — $2627.81, accounting for two-thirds of cocoa farmers' household income. In addition, illegal mining activities have also affected cocoa farmlands, impacting over 81% of cocoa farms in the Eastern region.

Cocoa trees with ripe pods. Source: *thebftonline.com*

From all indications, the earnings of cocoa farmers are a far cry from the revenue cocoa generates for Western companies and economies. Jointly, Ghana and Ivory Coast produce two-thirds of the world's cocoa. Sadly, cocoa farmers from the two countries continue to wallow in poverty even though their toil continues to sustain the economies of Western countries.

It is estimated that the UK chocolate industry is worth £ 3.96 billion, and sales of chocolate have seen a global upsurge — with forecasts of an estimated 35% increase in sales over the next five years. Overall, the global chocolate market size was valued at US$ 130.56 billion in 2019 and is expected to grow at a compound annual growth rate (CAGR) of 4.6% from 2020 to 2027 (Reuters 2019).

Unfortunately, out of this huge global cocoa revenue, Ghana receives only US$ 2 billion from syndicated loans for purchasing beans for export. Conversely, the United States of America alone makes over US$ 40 billion annually in retail sales of chocolate and cocoa products. In contrast, Ghanaian and Ivorian cocoa farmers accrued only 5.5% of the global supply chain, worth more than US$ 103 billion. This is even less than 15% of the government's revenue, a value-added tax on the sale of chocolate products in Western countries, where chocolate is consumed massively.

The unfair global world economic order and trade restrictions make it impossible for 'made in Ghana chocolate' or finished cocoa products to enter any Western market. The West is only interested in importing raw cocoa beans as part of an ideological strategy to keep Africa the producer and supplier of raw materials.

Estimates show that if Ghana's chocolate had a mere 1% access to European markets, Ghana would earn more than $ 5 billion annually. Undoubtedly, the trade restriction on finished cocoa products to Europe is a daunting challenge confronting President Akufo-Addo as Ghana embarks on this global economic renewal in 2021.

Historically, Ghana's first president, Dr. Kwame Nkrumah, attempted to regulate the cocoa market by building storage facilities to process and store cocoa beans. Through the storage, Nkrumah had hoped to dictate the global supply and price of cocoa for the local economy's benefit. Ideologically, this policy did not go down well with the European powers and was probably one of the reasons. Western powers were complicit in overthrowing Kwame Nkrumah.

In 2021, Ghana's President Nana Addo Dankwa Akufo-Addo took the boldest economic step in recent memory by announcing that Ghana will no longer export raw cocoa to Switzerland — and, perhaps, other Western countries. Rather, the world's second-largest cocoa producer will increase cocoa processing and chocolate production for export.

This move supports the notion that Africa has been marginalised in the international trade arena and needs to break that injustice. Ghana needs to move beyond primary commodity exports to value addition, especially converting cocoa into finished and semi-finished products for exports.

In 2021, Ghana and Ivory Coast threatened to withhold cocoa sales to United States manufacturers — accusing U.S. confectionary giants Hershey's and Mars of declining to pay a bonus meant to improve the economic fortunes of poor farmers. The Coffee Cocoa Council (CCC) and the Ghana Cocoa Board (Cocobod), in a statement, said two of the world's top chocolate sellers were not paying the living income differential (LID).

The LID gives cocoa farmers a bonus of US$400 per tonne in addition to the market price and is envisioned to cushion poor cocoa farmers' income. The two biggest West African cocoa producers successfully negotiated the US$400 a tonne LID on cocoa sales for the 2020/2021 season.

According to Bloomberg and Reuters, over the past two years, the price of a tonne of cocoa has dropped from US$3,000 to a little over US$1,900 in two years — even though there has been a significant rise in cash crop production. This development has affected the economic activities of cocoa farmers since their incomes have decreased by 30-40% as recorded by the Cocoa Barometer in 2018.

The decline in the price of cocoa has been a major problem for cocoa farmers of the two biggest producers, Ivory Coast and Ghana, as the two economies have suffered revenue reversals. In the interim, the International Monetary Fund (IMF) cautioned the two countries to reduce the domestic price of cocoa to reflect the drop in the price of cocoa on the international market. The Ghana government rejected the caution from the IMF and increased the producers' prices.

Ghanaian governments have identified inadequate processing as a challenge to producer countries. Sadly, for many decades, cocoa has been exported from Africa in its raw form. This is perhaps the reason Ghana, Ivory Coast, Nigeria, and Cameroon have been unable to receive an equitable share of global cocoa revenue. On the other hand, the European market accounts for about 50% of the global retail sales for chocolate.

In 2017, the European cocoa-processing industry experienced an increase of 1.3 million tonnes, representing 2.6%, and exported $20.6 billion of chocolate products. Within this period, cocoa-producing countries in Africa continued to experience negative impacts from the huge drop in price for cocoa. This is ample justification for Ghana, Ivory Coast, Nigeria, and Cameroon to invest in cocoa processing to accrue enough revenue from the cash crop, and possibly break the western monopoly over cocoa processing.

The Ghana Cocoa Processing Company currently has an installed capacity of a mere 25,000 tonnes. The government is investing in-plant expansion to increase the processing capacity from 25,000 to 65,000 tonnes of cocoa beans annually. Increased cocoa processing is even more critical if Ghana is to take advantage of the Africa Continental Free Trade Area Agreement (AfCFTA). AfCFTA offers the biggest opportunity for Ghana to supply premium cocoa products to the continent. Much as increased cocoa processing is meant to boost local industrialisation and job creation, it is also the surest means to ensure Ghana gets a fair share of the global cocoa revenue.

Cocoa processing companies in Ghana operate in an export zone called the Ghana Free Zones, which incentivises firms that export a minimum of 70% of their products. They are also eligible for tax exemptions on raw materials and machinery imports.

Among the cocoa processing factories in Ghana are top global cocoa processors Barry Callebaut, Cargill, and Olam. Only two Ghanaian-owned factories, the state-dominated Cocoa Processing Company (Golden Tree brand) and Niche Cocoa, make chocolate for domestic consumers. In addition, despite the tax burden, small-scale artisan chocolate makers, including 57 Chocolate, Midunu Chocolates, and Omama Royal Chocolate, have emerged.

Ghana has made remarkable progress in expanding its primary cocoa processing and chocolate production capacity. Now it is time to develop a vibrant domestic chocolate industry and benefit from a 1.3 billion strong market provided by the African Continental Free Trade Area.

6.1. GHANA'S REGIONAL AND GLOBAL LEADERSHIP

Ghana's regional and global leadership in areas such as peacekeeping, conflict resolution, and human rights advocacy

Ghana, as a country, has played a significant role in regional and global leadership in areas such as peacekeeping, conflict resolution, and human rights advocacy. Ghana's contribution to peacekeeping operations has been significant, with the country deploying troops to various African countries as part of peacekeeping missions. Ghana was among the first countries to contribute troops to the United Nations peacekeeping mission in Congo in 1960. Since then, Ghana has contributed to peacekeeping operations in Liberia, Sierra Leone, South Sudan, and many other countries.

In addition to peacekeeping, Ghana has played a critical role in conflict resolution in the West African region. For instance, in 2010, Ghana played a vital role in resolving the conflict between Ivory Coast's Laurent Gbagbo and Alassane Ouattara, leading to the former's arrest and the latter's presidential election. Ghana also played a role in resolving the Togo political crisis in 2005 and the Guinea political crisis in 2009.

Furthermore, Ghana has been a leading advocate for human rights in Africa. The country has ratified various international human rights conventions, including the International Covenant on Civil and Political Rights and the Convention on the Rights of the Child. Ghana's Constitution also guarantees various human rights, including freedom of expression, the right to a fair trial, and the right to education.

In recent years, Ghana has taken steps to enhance its regional and global leadership role in these areas. For instance, in 2018 Ghana hosted the African Union (AU) Extraordinary Summit on the African Continental Free Trade Area (AfCFTA) to promote intra-African trade and economic integration. Ghana has also been a leading voice in the call for the UN Security Council's reform, advocating for Africa's permanent seat on the council.

In conclusion, Ghana's regional and global leadership in peacekeeping, conflict resolution, and human rights advocacy has been significant. Ghana's contribution to peacekeeping operations has been critical in promoting peace and stability in various African countries. Furthermore, Ghana's role in conflict resolution has helped to resolve conflicts and promote peace in the West African region. Finally, Ghana's advocacy for human rights has helped to promote and protect the rights of its citizens and people across the African continent.

6.2. GHANA'S ECONOMIC GROWTH AND DEVELOPMENT

Ghana's economic growth and development have been heavily influenced by the government's implementation of various economic policies and programs. In the early 2000s, Ghana implemented various reforms to stabilise the economy, reduce inflation, and promote private-sector investment. These efforts helped create a more favourable environment for businesses, contributing to economic growth.

Ghana has a rich endowment of natural resources, including gold, cocoa, and timber, which have played a significant role in driving economic growth. However, the overreliance on natural resources has posed significant challenges to the country's economic development, with fluctuations in commodity prices leading to volatile growth patterns. The discovery of oil in 2007 further boosted Ghana's economy, leading to an increase in government revenue and the establishment of new industries.

In addition to natural resources, Ghana has made significant strides in other sectors, such as agriculture, manufacturing, and services. The agricultural sector remains a critical component of the economy, with cocoa significantly contributing to Ghana's economy. The government has also implemented various policies to promote the manufacturing and services sectors, aiming to diversify the economy.

Ghana's economy has been growing at a fast pace in recent years. According to the US Agency for International Development (USAID), Ghana has one of the fastest-growing economies in the world. Ghana's annual economic growth continued on a strong path at 6.3% in 2018, although slower than 8.1% in 2017. The country's GDP growth rate was 5.0% in 2021, up from 0.4% in 2020. However, Ghana's long-term economic growth is challenged by high energy costs; high levels of government debt, including in the energy sector; low access to credit; high borrowing costs; low agricultural productivity; a business climate restricting private sector growth; and regional trade barriers.

Disparities also exist between the country's North and South. Nearly 68% of Ghanaians in the Northern Region live on less than $1.25 a day, and stunting growth rates among children under five are as high as 40% in some regional districts.

Ghana has recently addressed these challenges through various initiatives to promote inclusive economic growth and development. The government has implemented various social intervention programs, such as the Livelihood Empowerment Against Poverty (LEAP), to support vulnerable groups.

Ghana has made significant strides in promoting economic growth and reducing poverty, with a decline in the poverty rate from 39.5% in 1992 to 23.4% in 2016. Additionally, the government has invested in infrastructure development, including roads, ports, and energy, to facilitate economic growth and development.

According to the African Development Bank's African Economic Outlook report, Ghana is expected to have one of the fastest-growing economies on the continent in 2024. With a predicted GDP growth of 5.1% in 2023, Ghana is outpacing the African average of 4.1%.

This growth is expected to be driven by several factors, including the government's COVID-19 Alleviation and Revitalisation of Enterprises Support Program and its 2023 budget, which aims to increase domestic revenue and reduce the country's dependence on borrowing.

The budget will also increase allocations to the Livelihood Empowerment Against Poverty (LEAP) payment per beneficiary household, which will help lift more people out of poverty and boost the country's overall prosperity.

In addition to these initiatives, the government is reducing spending to improve the country's fiscal position. For example, fuel allocation to political appointees and their heads will be cut by 50%, the use of large-engine vehicles within the city will be banned, and the purchase of vehicles will be limited to locally assembled ones. These measures will help to reduce unnecessary expenditures and allow the government to redirect funds towards more productive uses.

There are also several specific developments taking place in the private sector that could contribute to Ghana's economic success in 2023. For example, the Jospong Group of Companies has partnered with a major rice-producing company in Thailand to develop an integrated rice farming project in Ghana. If this project is successful, it could help end the need for rice imports into the country, which would be a major economic win for Ghana.

Another major development to watch out for in 2023 is the expected arrival of the first gold-for-oil shipments, which will eliminate the need for the country to spend $400m per month on fuel imports. This will save Ghana a significant amount of money and reduce the country's reliance on foreign sources of fuel, which will be a major boost to the economy.

Additionally, the Tema Oil Refinery is expected to resume operations in 2023, which could lead to more local fuel supply and a drop in fuel prices. This will be welcome news to consumers who have recently had to contend with high fuel prices.

In addition to these developments, it's worth noting that Fitch Solutions is predicting a stronger cedi against the major foreign currencies in 2024. According to its latest analysis of Ghana's 2024 Economic Outlook, it said the likely programme from the International Monetary Fund (IMF) signals to investors that the government is committed to fiscal consolidation that will turn around the economic predicament.

Overall, there are many good reasons for Ghanaians to be hopeful about their country's economic prospects in 2023/24. With a growing GDP, a commitment to fiscal consolidation, and a number of specific initiatives and developments taking place, there is much to be optimistic about in the public and private sectors.

That being said, it's important to recognize that achieving economic growth and prosperity doesn't happen automatically. It requires hard work, determination, and a willingness to take calculated risks and make the necessary investments to create a better future.

In other words, several positive developments are undoubtedly on the horizon that suggest Ghana is well-positioned for economic growth in the coming years. It's up to all of us — government officials, business leaders, and ordinary citizens — to work together and do our part to ensure this growth becomes a reality.

Ghana's economic growth and development trajectory provide significant lessons for other African countries. The country's commitment to promoting macroeconomic stability, investing in infrastructure development, and diversifying the economy has contributed to significant economic growth and poverty reduction. However, the country still faces significant challenges in addressing inequality, promoting sustainable economic growth, and promoting job creation.

6.3. GHANA'S GOVERNMENT'S POLICIES TO PROMOTE ECONOMIC GROWTH AND DEVELOPMENT

Ghana's government has implemented various policies to promote economic growth and development over the years. These policies have improved the business environment, promoted private sector growth, and attracted foreign investment. Some of the policies include:

Economic Recovery Program (ERP): This program was launched in 1983 to address the country's economic crisis. The ERP aimed to stabilize the economy, reduce inflation, and promote private sector growth. It involved measures such as the devaluation of the currency, removal of subsidies, and privatization of state-owned enterprises.

National Export Strategy (NES): This policy was launched in 1995 to promote non-traditional exports and diversify the country's export base. The NES aimed to increase export earnings, create jobs, and reduce the country's dependence on a few export commodities.

Ghana Poverty Reduction Strategy (GPRS): This policy was launched in 2003 to address poverty and inequality. The GPRS aimed to reduce poverty, promote economic growth, and improve social services such as education and health. It involved increased investment in agriculture, infrastructure, and human capital development.

Ghana Shared Growth and Development Agenda (GSGDA): This policy was launched in 2010 to promote inclusive growth and development. The GSGDA aimed to create jobs, reduce poverty, and promote private sector growth. It involved improving the business environment, investing in infrastructure, and promoting agribusiness.

One District, One Factory (1D1F): This policy was launched in 2017 to promote industrialization and job creation at the district level. The 1D1F aimed to create at least one factory in each district to promote local economic development and reduce unemployment.

Planting for Food and Jobs (PFJ): This policy was launched in 2017 to promote agricultural productivity and food security. The PFJ aimed to increase agricultural productivity, create jobs, and reduce the country's dependence on food imports. It involved measures such as providing subsidized inputs and extension services to farmers.

In addition, the government has implemented various policies to promote private sector growth and attract foreign investment. These include tax incentives for investors, establishing special economic zones, and implementing business-friendly regulations. The government has also invested heavily in infrastructure development, including roads, ports, and airports, to facilitate economic growth and development.

Despite these efforts, Ghana still faces significant challenges in poverty reduction and addressing inequality. The country has high levels of income inequality, with the richest 10% of the population owning more than 40% of the country's wealth. The government needs to continue to implement targeted policies and programs to address these challenges and ensure that all Ghanaians have access to basic needs such as education, healthcare, and social protection.

6.4. GHANA'S GROWING MIDDLE CASS

Ghana has experienced significant growth in its middle class in recent years. This emerging middle class is characterised by individuals who can consume beyond their basic needs and can afford to invest in assets such as education, health, housing, and other amenities. This group is also considered a key driver of economic growth and development in the country.

One of the main factors contributing to the growth of Ghana's middle class is the country's sustained economic growth over the past two decades. This has led to the creation of more jobs, particularly in the services and manufacturing sectors, which has improved the standard of living for many Ghanaians. In addition, the country has implemented policies that promote social welfare and economic empowerment, which have further enhanced the growth of the middle class.

The Ghanaian government has recognized the potential of the growing middle class and has implemented policies to support its growth. One of the key policies is the development of the private sector, which has created more job opportunities and entrepreneurial opportunities for the middle class. The government has also implemented policies aimed at promoting education, which has increased the human capital of the middle class, making them more productive and competitive in the labour market.

Moreover, the government has also implemented policies to reduce poverty and inequality, which have benefited the middle class. These policies include targeted social welfare programs such as free school feeding, free basic healthcare, and cash transfer programs for the poor and vulnerable. In addition, the government has initiated policies to promote gender equality and women's empowerment, contributing to the growth of the middle class, particularly among women.

However, despite the growth of the middle class in Ghana, challenges still exist. Income inequality remains high, and many Ghanaians still struggle to meet their basic needs. Furthermore, the middle class is still relatively small compared to the overall population, and there is a need for more policies and programs to support its growth.

In conclusion, Ghana's growing middle class can potentially drive economic growth and development. The government has recognized this potential and has implemented policies to support its growth. However, more needs to be done to address the challenges of poverty and inequality and to promote the growth of the middle class.

6.5. GHANAIAN DIASPORA

Ghana is one of few African countries with a bigger and more dispersed diaspora even though actual figures of Ghanaians living abroad are still unknown due to factors such as varying definitions of "diaspora" and the fluid nature of migration due to data inconsistencies and the soaring rate of irregular migration out of the country. The estimates provided by Ghanaian Missions Abroad show that Ghanaians reside in some 53 countries.

According to the International Organization for Migration (IOM), as of 2020, an estimated 2.6 million Ghanaians were living abroad. The largest concentrations of the Ghanaian diaspora are found in countries such as the United States, the United Kingdom, Canada, Germany, and the Netherlands. These estimates include Ghanaians who migrated for economic opportunities, education, or other reasons and those born to Ghanaian parents abroad.

The Ghanaian diaspora is dynamic, with individuals moving between countries and new generations being born in diaspora communities. There are also significant numbers of Ghanaian migrants within the West African region, particularly in countries such as Nigeria, Cote d'Ivoire, and Burkina Faso, where economic opportunities and regional integration often drive migration flows.

The diaspora plays a significant role in Ghana across various aspects of the country's development, including economic, social, and cultural contributions. Here are some key roles and contributions of the diaspora in Ghana:

Remittances: Ghanaians living abroad, particularly in countries like the United States, United Kingdom, and Canada, send remittances back to their families and communities in Ghana. The World Bank Migration and Development Report for 2021 has reported an increase of 5 per cent to $3.6 billion in remittance flows to Ghana despite the global lockdowns in the heat of the COVID-19 pandemic. These remittances serve as an important source of income and financial support, contributing to poverty reduction, education, healthcare, and overall economic stability.

Investment and Entrepreneurship: The Ghanaian diaspora actively engages in investment and entrepreneurship in Ghana. Many individuals and organizations leverage their knowledge, skills, and resources to establish businesses, create employment opportunities, and contribute to economic growth. Diaspora investments span sectors such as real estate, manufacturing, agriculture, technology, and services.

Knowledge and Skills Transfer: Ghanaians in the diaspora often possess valuable expertise, qualifications, and experiences gained from living and working abroad. They contribute to knowledge and skills transfer through collaborations, mentorship programs, and partnerships with local institutions, businesses, and organizations. This helps to enhance capacity, innovation, and professional development in Ghana.

Philanthropy and Development Initiatives: The Ghanaian diaspora actively supports philanthropic and development initiatives in Ghana. It contributes to social causes, education, healthcare, infrastructure projects, and community development through charitable donations, volunteering, and participation in non-profit organizations. These efforts have a positive impact on various sectors and communities within Ghana.

Cultural Preservation and Promotion: The diaspora plays a vital role in preserving and promoting Ghanaian culture, traditions, and heritage. Ghanaians abroad often organize cultural events, festivals, and exhibitions to showcase Ghanaian arts, music, dance, and cuisine. They also contribute to the preservation of local languages, traditional practices, and historical knowledge.

Brain Gain and Return Migration: Some diaspora members choose to return to Ghana permanently or temporarily, bringing with them valuable skills, experiences, and connections gained abroad. Their return contributes to human capital development, innovation, and the transfer of global best practices to various sectors in Ghana.

The Ghanaian diaspora is a valuable and diverse resource for the country, playing a crucial role in driving economic growth, social development, cultural preservation, and global connections. The Ghanaian government and various organizations actively seek to engage and harness the potential of the diaspora through initiatives such as the Diaspora Engagement Policy, Diaspora Bonds, and investment promotion programs.

7. Ghana's Natural Resources

The West African county of Ghana has been blessed with large mineral deposits since the 16th century. However, it is only recently that new technology has made it possible to locate mineral deposits quickly, attracting numerous international companies' interest in Ghana. The Mining Industry in Ghana contributes to about 5% of the country's GDP, while minerals make up approximately 37% of total global exports. Ghana has 23 mines that excavate minerals such as diamonds, bauxite, gold, and manganese.

There are also 300 registered small-scale mining groups and 90 mine support service companies. In this section, we will look at the ten mineral resources in Ghana, their location, and their use in the country.

Ghana Gold. Source: *www.azureviral.com*

Gold

Ghana is the largest gold producer in Africa and the 7th largest producer globally, with an annual production of about 4.5 million ounces. Gold has been a major contributor to Ghana's economy, accounting for about 42% of the country's total exports.

Gold deposits in Ghana are primarily found in the Birimian rocks, which span the country's southwest and northeast regions. These rocks are part of the West African Craton and are known for their gold-bearing potential.

Gold is generally used to make jewellery but can also be used to make coins, for dentistry, and even has applications in the aerospace industry. Even though yellow gold is the most known form of gold, white gold (a mixture of gold, palladium silver, and nickel) also exists in some parts of Ghana and is used for bridal jewellery. Ghana has attracted significant foreign investment in large-scale gold mining operations. Mining companies such as AngloGold Ashanti, Newmont Mining Corporation, and Gold Fields Limited have established mines in the country, employing modern mining techniques and technologies. In addition to large-scale mining, Ghana has a thriving artisanal and small-scale mining sector (ASM). ASM involves informal mining activities carried out by individuals or small groups using rudimentary tools and techniques.

The gold industry has created employment opportunities, especially in rural areas where most of the population resides. However, the mining activities have also resulted in environmental degradation, land use disputes, and conflicts between mining companies and local communities. The primary gold deposits in Ghana are in Obuasi, Damang, Prestea, Tarkwa, Abosa, Bogoso, and Bibiani.

Petroleum and Natural Gas

Ghanaians have been drilling for oil for quite some time; in 2008, Kosmos Energy LLC struck liquid gold, and production started in 2010. Commercial oil production in Ghana began in 2010 after the discovery of the offshore Jubilee Field, which is one of the largest oil fields in West Africa. Since then, additional oil fields, such as the Tweneboa-Enyenra-Ntomme (TEN) Field and the Sankofa-Gye Nyame Field have also been developed. Most of Ghana's petroleum reserves are located offshore in the Gulf of Guinea. International oil companies operate offshore fields, including Tullow Oil, Kosmos Energy, and Eni. These companies employ advanced technology and expertise to extract oil and gas from beneath the seabed.

Alongside oil, Ghana has significant natural gas reserves. Natural gas is formed through sedimentary and metamorphic actions on marine plants and animal remains. As the remains are buried deep underground, heat changes their composition to oil and gas deposits over many years. Natural gas is also extracted at the oilfields where crude oil is drilled. Some oilfields that extract natural gas are the Jubilee and Saltpond oilfields, which average about 2 million cubic feet of natural gas per day.

Natural gas associated with oil production is utilized for domestic consumption, electricity generation, and industrial applications. The government has implemented measures to encourage the development of natural gas infrastructure and promote using natural gas as an alternative to more polluting fuels.

Ghana's oil production has steadily increased, contributing to the country's economic growth. Ghana is believed to have about 5 billion to 7 billion barrels of crude oil in its reserves, making it the 6th largest oil reserve in Africa and the 25th in the world. Crude oil is one of the base materials for transportation fuels like diesel, kerosene, jet fuel, and gasoline, and it is additionally used for electricity generation and heating. The most common oilfields in Ghana include Jubilee Oilfields, Joy Oilfields, and Butask Oil Fields.

Ghana has established regulatory bodies to oversee the petroleum sector, including the Ministry of Energy, the Ghana National Petroleum Corporation (GNPC), and the Petroleum Commission. These entities are responsible for managing licenses, enforcing regulations, and ensuring transparency and accountability in the industry. Ghana has also emphasized the importance of local content development in the petroleum sector. Efforts are being made to increase local participation, promote skills development, and enhance the capabilities of Ghanaian businesses to provide goods and services to the industry.

The oil sector has contributed significantly to Ghana's economy, with oil exports accounting for about 10% of the country's total exports. The sector has also created jobs and attracted foreign investment.

Manganese

Consmin is a company that owns about 90% of the Ghana Manganese Companies. Manganese is often used as an alloy to make other metals, like steel, because it is too brittle to function as a pure metal. It can be found in the ground as ore in two different forms: oxides and carbonate. Seven regions in Ghana are filled with deposits of this mineral. They are the Upper-West, Ashanti, Western, Northern, Central, Upper-East, and Eastern. The primary deposits are at Nsuta in the Western Region.

Diamonds

Diamonds are among the most valuable stones globally; only a lucky handful of nations can access deposits. However, Ghana is fortunate since the country has more than 11 million carats of diamond reserves located seventy miles to the North West of Accra. It is mainly mined at Akwatia in the Birim and Bonza diamond fields.

Ghana currently produces approximately one million carats of diamonds per year, making the country the 9th largest diamond producer globally. Diamonds are primarily used to make jewellery and cutting and drilling equipment.

Bauxite

Bauxite is one of the most common minerals in the earth's crust and its ore is rich in aluminium. Ghana has about 554 million metric tons of bauxite reserves; it is used in the petroleum, chemical, abrasive, refractory, steel, and cement industries. Furthermore, Bauxite deposits can be found in Ashanti and the Western and Eastern regions. The four major deposit sites are Kibi, Aya-Nyinahin, Ejuanema, and Sefwi — Bekwai.

Iron

Iron ore is in high demand due to its applications in population and infrastructure growth in almost every country. Iron ore is typically processed to form steel, which has countless benefits, such as building beams, furniture, locomotives, and reinforcing rods for concrete.

Ghana's three significant iron ore deposits are located at Oppong Mansi, Shieni, and Pudo. Similarly, some iron mining companies in Ghana include Maurla Mines Ghana Ltd, Gold

Coast Resources Ltd, Minergy Resources Ltd, and Inland Ghana Mines Limited.

Salt

The salt production potential is enormous since Ghana's coast faces the Gulf of Guinea and its coastline stretches for about 500km. Ghana produces between 250,000 to 300,000 tons of salt annually, despite its production potential of 2.2 million tons annually. The primary way of extracting salt in Ghana is by "Solar Evaporation" (using the sun's heat to evaporate the salty water, leaving only the ice crystals).

Salt is one of the most in-demand mineral resources globally, with its uses spanning domestic to industrial purposes.

Limestone

Limestone is one of the main ingredients used to make cement. Deposits can be found at Oterkpolu, Nauli, Buipe, and Bongo-Da. Ghana is estimated to have over 230 million tons of limestone reserves. The GHACEM limestone quarry at Yongwa, established in 2014, is one of the biggest in Ghana. Apart from being a significant ingredient in cement, limestone is used in toothpaste, food additives, and raw material in the chemical industry.

Dolomite

The Buipe-Baka, in the Northern region, holds the highest dolomite deposit in Ghana. Dolomite is used in the chemical industry as an additive for livestock, a soil conditioner, and an ingredient in glass, ceramics, and bricks.

Conclusion

These are the top 10 mineral resources and where they are mined in Ghana. Ghana is rich in many mineral resources and takes advantage of this to boost its economy. However, Ghana has an array of untapped mineral resources; a few, like crude oil and iron, were recently stumbled upon.

Therefore, numerous global companies come into the country and spend millions of dollars researching the ground to discover other valuable minerals.

7.1. THE TOP CROPS OF GHANA AND THEIR IMPORTANCE

"Agriculture not only gives riches to a nation but the only riches she can call her own." — Samuel Johnson.

Cocoa

Cocoa is probably the most economically important crop in Ghana. The cocoa plant was introduced in Ghana in 1870 by Tetteh Quarshie. Today, Ghana is the second largest exporter of cocoa in the world. Cocoa is the second-largest export commodity in Ghana, with an annual production of about 900,000 metric tons, accounting for about 19% of the country's total exports. The cocoa sector has played a critical role in Ghana's economy, providing employment opportunities for farmers and creating income for rural communities.

Cocoa is cultivated in the country's southern parts and frequently by small-scale farmers. However, the sale and export of cocoa is highly regulated. All farmers must sell their harvest to the Ghana Cocoa Board (Cocobod), which then sells to companies for export.

Growing cocoa is an exercise in patience, and it takes 10-15 years for a tree to reach peak production. Also, there is usually only one harvest in October.

In 2019-2020, cocoa production was just under 1 million metric tons. However, comparing Ghana's per-hectare production to other countries, it seems like farmers in Ghana are not making the most of their plantations.

Pineapple

There are three main varieties of pineapples: sugarloaf, smooth cayenne, and MD2. The sugarloaf variety is conical and generally only sold in Ghana's local markets. For a long time, smooth cayenne dominated the international export market. However, Costa Rica introduced the MD2 to the international market, and because of its bright yellow colour and square shape, it became the preferred variety by supermarkets.

The MD2 variety isn't particularly well-suited for Ghana's growing conditions; however, the smooth cayenne variety is better for juicing. While Ghana dominated the European pineapple markets until the early 2000s, producers are trying to shift their focus to companies interested in juice production.

Palm Oil

Unlike Southeast Asia, where palm production is growing at such a rate that it is destroying the habitats of a number of animals, palm oil is a culturally important part of the diet in Ghana and West Africa. Palm oil trees are grown in various regions of Ghana, with the Ashanti, Western, and Central regions being the major palm oil production areas. Smallholder farmers, as well as large-scale plantations, engage in palm oil cultivation. Smallholder farmers play a significant role in palm oil production in Ghana. They cultivate palm oil trees on their land and typically process the harvested fruits into palm oil using traditional methods. In addition to these small farms, there are also large-scale plantations and agribusiness companies involved in palm oil production. These operations employ modern farming techniques, machinery, and processing facilities to enhance productivity and efficiency.

Palm oil is a versatile product used in various ways. In Ghana, it is commonly used for cooking and as an ingredient in traditional dishes. Additionally, palm oil is used in the food processing industry for products such as margarine, cooking oil, and snacks. The expansion of palm oil plantations has raised concerns about deforestation and biodiversity loss in some areas. However, Ghana has implemented regulations and initiatives to promote sustainable palm oil production, including protecting forest reserves and promoting responsible land management practices.

Ghana does export palm oil. More than 2.5 million metric tons were produced in 2014-2015 (it fetches a lower price per ton than cocoa).

Sugarcane

Walking along the street, you might find a row of sugar cane leaning up against a small fence. You can easily buy some to be chopped up for you to chew on as a snack. Sugarcane cultivation and production in Ghana have historically been limited compared to other crops. However, there are ongoing efforts to develop the sugarcane industry in the country. Here are some key points about sugarcane in Ghana: The cultivation of sugarcane is primarily concentrated in specific regions, including parts of the Volta and Central regions. Small farmers typically grow sugarcane as a cash crop alongside other crops, such as maize or cassava, to diversify their income sources. The Komenda Sugar Factory in the Central Region was established to promote local sugar production and reduce the country's reliance on sugar imports.

Expanding the sugarcane industry has the potential to create employment opportunities, especially in rural areas. It can contribute to rural development, poverty reduction, and income generation for farmers and associated stakeholders. Sugarcane can also be used for ethanol production.

7.2. GHANA EXPORT

The Republic of Ghana shipped an estimated $12.75 billion worth of goods around the globe in 2021, an 9.5% decrease compared to the $14.1 billion worth of exported goods in 2020.

Ghana's top five exported products are crude oil, gold, cocoa beans, cocoa paste, cocoa butter, fats and oils. These key product categories represent almost 80% of Ghana's revenues from exporting goods during 2021.

Major Trade Partners Importing Ghana's Exports

More than 80% of products exported from Ghana were bought by importers from China (16.7% of Ghana's global total), Switzerland (14.7%), India (14.2%), South Africa (11.8%), Netherlands (5.8%), United Arab Emirates (5.4%), United States of America (4.2%), United Kingdom (2.5%), France (2.2%), Italy (1.84%), Japan (1.81%) and Burkina Faso (1.7%).

From a continental perspective, 43.4% of Ghana's exports by value were delivered to Asian countries, while 32.9% were sold to importers in Europe. Ghana shipped another 17.7% worth of goods to fellow African trade partners.

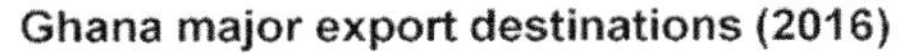

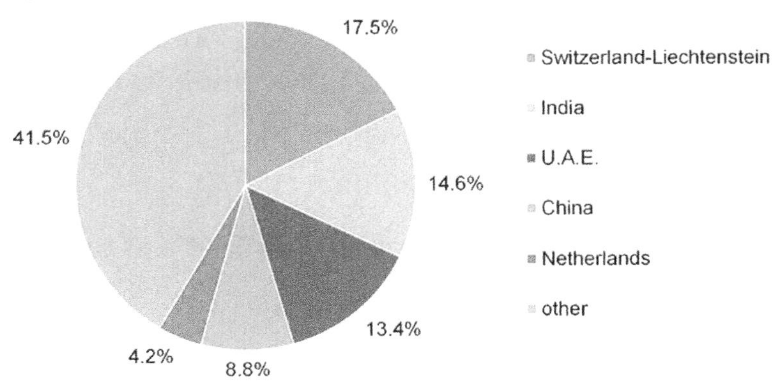

Ghana major export destination. Source: *Britanica.com*

Given Ghana's population of 31.3 million people, it's total $12.75 billion in 2021 exports translates to roughly $410 for every resident in the West African country. That dollar metric represents a modest increase from the average $400 per capita for 2020.

Ghana's Top 10 Exports

The following export product groups represent the highest dollar value in Ghanaian global shipments during 2021. Also shown is the percentage share each export category represents regarding overall exports from Ghana.

1. Mineral fuels, including oil: $4 billion
2. Gems, precious metals: $3.6 billion
3. Cocoa: $2.8 billion (22%)
4. Fruits, nuts: $440.5 million (3.5%)
5. Ores, slag, ash: $368.9 million (2.9%)

6. Animal/vegetable fats, oils, waxes: $212.5 million (1.7%)
7. Wood: $169.4 million (1.3%)
8. Rubber, rubber articles: $147.7 million (1.2%)
9. Meat/seafood preparations: $134.2 million (1.1%)
10. Aluminium: $128.7 million (1%)

Ghana's top 10 exports accounted for 94.4% of the overall value of its global shipments.

Crude oil is Ghana's most valuable export product (29.8% of Ghanaian exports). In second place was gold (28.1%) trailed by cocoa beans (14.3%), cocoa paste (3.8%), cocoa butter, fats and oils (2.7%), manganese ores or concentrates (2.3%), cashew nuts and coconuts (1.7%), natural rubber and similar gums (1.14%), prepared fish including caviar (1.05%), and then cocoa powder with no added sugar (1.02%).

Products Causing Ghana's Worst Trade Deficits

Overall, Ghana incurred an estimated -$5.7 billion product trade deficit for 2021. That deficit represents a 110.2% upturn from -$2.7 billion in red ink one year earlier.

Below are Ghana's imports that result in negative net exports or product trade balance deficits.

1. Machinery, including computers: -$2.1 billion (Up by 16.5% since 2020)
2. Vehicles: -$1.7 billion (Up by 13.9%)
3. Plastics, plastic articles: -$1.1 billion (Up by 25.5%)
4. Electrical machinery, equipment: -$1.1 billion (Down by -13.1%)
5. Iron, steel: -$839.7 million (Up by 7.2%)
6. Articles of iron or steel: -$631.3 million (Up by 7.7%)

7. Meat: -$537.7 million (Up by 50.7%)
8. Pharmaceuticals: -$453.7 million (Up by 48.4%)
9. Cereals: -$432.9 million (Down by -26.5%)
10. Furniture, bedding, lighting, signs, prefabricated buildings: -$370.5 million (Up by 12.8%)

Ghanaian Export Companies

Some exports-related companies from Ghana as:

- Accra Brewery Company (beer)
- African Champion Industries (paper)
- Aluworks (aluminium)
- Ayrton Drugs (pharmaceuticals)
- CFAO Ghana (automobiles)
- Cocoa Processing Company (cocoa beans)
- Ghana National Petroleum Corporation (oil, gas)
- Kuapa Kokoo (cocoa)
- Pioneer Kitchenware (household goods)
- Printex (textiles)

In macroeconomic terms, Ghana's total exported goods represent 6.6% of its overall Gross Domestic Product for 2021 ($193.8 billion valued in Purchasing Power Parity US dollars). That 6.6% for exports to overall GDP in PPP for 2021 compares to 6.5% for 2020. Those percentages suggest a relatively increasing reliance on products sold on international markets for Ghana's total economic performance, albeit based on a short timeframe.

Another key indicator of a country's economic performance is its unemployment rate. Ghana's unemployment rate is forecast to be 4.6% at the end of 2022, up from an average 4.5% in 2020 per Trading Economics.

7.3. GHANA'S AGRICULTURE EXPORT

In 2021 Ghana imported about $1.9 billion in agricultural and related products. Imports from the United States ($156.6 million) constituted about 8% of the total import value. Food and agricultural imports will continue to grow as Ghana's underdeveloped food processing sector cannot meet increasing demand. Food imports mostly comprise bulk, intermediate, and consumer-oriented commodities such as rice, wheat, soybean meal, and poultry. U.S. exports of agricultural and related products to Ghana in 2021 were $156.6 million, an increase of about 48.0% over the previous year's value ($105.6 million).

Ghana is strategically located and has been marketed to the rest of the world over the years as the gateway to Africa. Currently pursuing an agenda to make its seaports very competitive along the coasts of West Africa, Ghana provides a good transhipment point for food and beverages meant for the greater West Africa market. U.S. grocery items entering Ghana can be re-exported to neighbouring West African countries (a market of over 400 million people).

Ghana remains a major importer of food products, with imports of agricultural and related products estimated to have reached $1.9 billion in 2021.

With an estimated population of roughly 31 million, Ghana's market remains relatively advanced compared to others in Africa, despite the significant dip in economic growth recorded in recent years, mainly because of the impact of the COVID-19 pandemic. Rapid urbanization and gains in economic growth continue to stimulate an emerging middle class that embraces Western brands, products, and lifestyles.

Although U.S. exports to Ghana mostly consisted of rice, poultry, and wheat, exports of U.S. consumer-oriented food products reached an all-time high of $127.2 million in 2021. Based on year-over-year growth in 2021, the ten best U.S. high-value consumer-oriented product categories for the Ghanaian market are in descending order 1) beer; 2) chocolate and cocoa products; 3) pork and pork products; 4) beef and beef products; and 5) wine and related products; 6) food preparations; 7) seafood products; 8) non-alcoholic beverages; 9); fruit and vegetable juices; and 10) essential oils.

In descending order, the 2021 top 10 leading agricultural and related product suppliers to Ghana are China, Brazil, Netherlands, Malaysia, and Canada. The remaining suppliers are the United States, Turkey, India, Indonesia, and Belgium. Imports of consumer-oriented food from the European Union remain strong.

Opportunities in Ghana

- Growing middle-class driving consumption of high-value food products
- Demand for intermediate products due to the growing food processing industry
- Entry and growth of U.S. fast food franchises
- Relatively good infrastructure: ports, airport, and roads
- Consumers looking for ready-to-eat products as per capita income grows

- The country remains the ideal regional distribution logistics hub
- Growing tourism and corporate hotel industry

Ghana imports about 100,000 vehicles per year. About 90 per cent are used vehicles, with an estimated value of US$1.14 billion annually. The United States, Japan, and Germany are leading suppliers.

7.4. GHANA'S ECONOMIC GROWTH, DIVERSIFICATION, AND INDUSTRIALIZATION EFFORTS

Ghana's economic growth over the years has been driven by its natural resources, particularly gold, oil, and cocoa. However, the country has made significant efforts to diversify its economy and focus on industrialization to reduce its overreliance on these resources.

In the 1960s and 1970s, Ghana pursued an industrialization policy known as the "Industrial Promotion Services" (IPS) program. The program aimed to promote the development of the manufacturing sector through import substitution and the creation of employment opportunities. However, the program faced several challenges, including a lack of funding, inadequate infrastructure, and inefficiencies in managing state-owned enterprises.

In the 1980s, Ghana's economic policies shifted towards a market-oriented approach, introducing the Structural Adjustment Program (SAP). The SAP aimed to liberalize the economy, reduce government spending and debt, and encourage private sector growth. However, the program was criticized for its social and economic costs, including high inflation, unemployment, and reduced public spending on healthcare and education.

In recent years, Ghana has made significant efforts to diversify its economy, focusing on promoting the agricultural and manufacturing sectors. The government has launched various initiatives to support these sectors, including the "One District, One Factory" initiative, which aims to establish at least one factory in every district of the country to promote industrialization and job creation.

The country has also been working to improve its business environment and attract foreign investment. In 2013, Ghana launched the Ghana Investment Promotion Centre (GIPC), which is responsible for promoting and facilitating investment in the country. The GIPC has implemented various reforms to improve the ease of doing business in Ghana, including streamlining the process of registering a business and reducing the time and cost involved.

Ghana's political stability and democratic governance have also supported Ghana's economic growth. The country has held peaceful and transparent elections since the return to multi-party democracy in 1992. This stability has helped to attract foreign investment and create a conducive environment for economic growth.

Ghana has made significant progress in economic growth and development in the past few decades, but the country still faces significant challenges, particularly in poverty, inequality, and corruption; the country still faces significant challenges in achieving sustained economic growth and reducing poverty. Despite its efforts to diversify its economy, the country remains heavily reliant on its natural resources, particularly gold, oil, and cocoa. Promoting more value-added activities in these sectors is needed to increase their economic contribution.

Poverty remains a significant challenge in Ghana, with a large portion of the population living below the poverty line. The government has implemented various poverty reduction programs over the years, such as the Livelihood Empowerment Against Poverty (LEAP) program, which provides cash transfers to the poorest households in the country. The government has also implemented various social interventions, such as free primary education, to improve the living standards of Ghanaians.

Inequality remains a major challenge in Ghana, with significant disparities in income, education, and access to basic services between urban and rural areas and different regions. The government has implemented various policies and programs to address inequality, such as the Northern Development Authority, which aims to promote development in the northern regions of the country, where poverty and inequality are most acute.

Corruption is also a significant challenge in Ghana, ranking 75th out of 180 countries in the 2021 Corruption Perception Index. Corruption affects all aspects of life in Ghana, from the delivery of basic services to the business environment. The government has implemented various anti-corruption measures, such as establishing the Office of the Special Prosecutor, which is tasked with investigating and prosecuting corruption cases. However, the effectiveness of these measures is still a matter of debate.

These policies have made it easier for foreign investors to do business in Ghana, such as easing regulations and reducing taxes. The government has promoted the manufacturing sector by incentivising local manufacturers and attracting foreign investors. The manufacturing sector has been growing at an average rate of 10% annually, positively impacting the country's economy. The manufacturing sector has created jobs for thousands of Ghanaians and helped reduce the country's import dependence. Overall, Ghana has made significant economic development over the past few years. The country's economy has been growing at an impressive rate, and the government has implemented policies conducive to economic growth. Ghana has attracted foreign investment, and the manufacturing sector has grown steadily.

In 2018, Chinese telecommunications giant Huawei invested $5 million in Ghana to establish a rural network project. Doing so aimed to improve network coverage and internet connectivity in rural areas, which is expected to impact economic development in those regions positively.

The United Kingdom-Ghana Business Council (UKGBC) was established in 2019 to promote trade and investment between the two countries. The UKGBC aims to support UK businesses in Ghana and to help Ghanaian businesses export to the UK. One of the notable investments resulting from this partnership was the opening of the Ghana Bank of London in 2019, which aims to strengthen trade and business relationships between Ghana and the UK.

Kwabena Duffour Jr., a Ghanaian entrepreneur, founded the agri-tech firm AgroCenta in 2015. AgroCenta provides a platform connecting small-scale farmers with buyers, allowing them to sell their products easily. With support from the Ghanaian government and investors, AgroCenta has grown and currently operates in seven regions across Ghana, impacting over 22,000 farmers. This has helped to improve income levels, reduce post-harvest losses, and increase food security in the country.

The mobile money industry has experienced significant growth in Ghana, with active mobile money accounts reaching over 13 million in 2020. This growth has been facilitated by policies implemented by the government, including the introduction of mobile money regulations in 2015 and the launch of a universal QR code system in 2020. The mobile money sector has created jobs, increased financial inclusion, and improved access to financial services, positively impacting the country's economy.

In conclusion, while Ghana has made significant progress in economic growth and development, the country still faces significant challenges in poverty, inequality, and corruption. The government has implemented various policies and programs to address these challenges. Still, more needs to be done to ensure that all Ghanaians benefit from the country's economic growth and development.

7.5. GHANAIAN'S CONTRIBUTIONS TO THE WORLD

From ancient times to today, Ghanaians have contributed to various fields, including arts and culture, sports, politics, and economics. In this essay, we will explore some of the significant contributions made by Ghanaians to the world.

Ghana's Food and Drug Authority is the first country to approve a new malaria vaccine known as R21 from Oxford University, a potential step forward in fighting a disease that kills hundreds of thousands of children annually.

Peaceable country — Ghana was ranked as Africa's most peaceful country by the Global Index. The last military ruler was Jerry Rawlings, who ushered in multi-party democracy in the 1990s. Thenceforth, Ghana has experienced one of the rarest and most admirable stretches of peace in African history. It is one of the few African countries to have persistently held credible elections and experienced a peaceful transition from one president to another. It has spread these peace dividends to other parts of West Africa by mediating and bringing peace to conflict zones.

Largest open-air market — Ghana has the largest market in West Africa. It's called Kejetia market and it's located in Kumasi, the Ashanti region's capital. Kumasi is the famous capital of the Ashanti Kingdom, about 100 miles north of Accra, Ghana's capital city. Kumasi is famous for its ancient history as a gold trade centre. Kejetia market is well-known for its plentiful gold and diamond jewellery. Apart from jewellery, the famous Ashanti Kente traditional clothing fabric dots most of its garment shops.

Kejetia market. Source: *www.lonelyplanet.com*

Most tourists are attracted to the Kejetia market due to the ability to have an interactive experience with locals in a busy market yet be able to find and buy authentic cultural artefacts. With almost 50,000 stores concentrated in one area, you are spoilt for variety in your shopping experience.

Economics — Ghana's economy has undergone significant transformation in recent years, and Ghanaians have played a significant role in this process. The country has produced several prominent economists, including George Ayittey and Kwesi Botchwey. Ayittey is a renowned economist and author who has written extensively on Africa's challenges and the need for economic reform. Botchwey, on the other hand, served as Ghana's finance minister in the 1980s and played a significant role in stabilizing the country's economy.

Art — One of the most celebrated Ghanaian artists is El Anatsui, whose works have been featured in galleries and museums worldwide. Anatsui's art is made from discarded objects, such as bottle caps, copper wire, and aluminium cans, which he transforms into large-scale, visually stunning sculptures. His work addresses themes like identity, history, and social commentary and has been praised for its innovation and creativity.

Another notable Ghanaian artist is Ibrahim Mahama, who uses jute sacks, a common material used for carrying goods in Ghana, to create large-scale installations and sculptures. Mahama's work addresses issues of globalization, trade, and the legacy of colonialism. His works have been featured in major exhibitions and biennials across the world.

Science — Ghana has produced several notable scientists who have significantly contributed to their fields. One such individual is Professor Francis Allotey, a mathematician and physicist known for his groundbreaking work in mathematical physics.

Allotey developed the "Allotey Formalism," a mathematical technique for analysing atoms and molecules. He was the first African to be awarded the Prince Philip Gold Medal in 1973.

Another notable Ghanaian scientist is Professor Dorothy Yeboah-Manu, a microbiologist who has significantly contributed to tuberculosis research. Yeboah-Manu's work has helped identify and understand the transmission of drug-resistant tuberculosis strains in Ghana and across the world. She has received numerous awards for her work, including the prestigious Kwame Nkrumah Scientific Award in 2016.

Technology — Ghana has also produced several notable individuals in the technology field. One such person is Herman Chinery-Hesse, the "Bill Gates of Africa." Chinery-Hesse is a software entrepreneur and co-founder of SOFTtribe, one of the largest software companies in West Africa. He has been recognized for promoting technology and entrepreneurship in Africa and has received numerous awards, including the World Economic Forum's "Global Leader for Tomorrow" award.

Another notable Ghanaian in the technology field is Regina Honu, a social entrepreneur and founder of Soronko Solutions, which provides technology training and services to young people, especially girls and women. Honu has been recognized for promoting women's empowerment through technology and has received numerous awards, including the "African Digital Woman of the Year" award in 2016.

In conclusion, Ghana has produced many notable individuals in art, science, and technology whose contributions have had a significant impact on Ghana and the global stage. These individuals have demonstrated exceptional talent and creativity and used their skills and knowledge to address important social and scientific issues.

7.6. NOTABLE GHANAIANS ON THE WORLD SCENE

Ghana has produced several notable individuals who have significantly contributed to various fields on the world stage. Here are some Ghanaians who have achieved great success and recognition in their respective fields:

Kofi Annan: Kofi Annan was a Ghanaian diplomat who served as the seventh Secretary-General of the United Nations from 1997 to 2006. He was the first black African to hold the position and was awarded the Nobel Peace Prize in 2001 for his work on peacekeeping and human rights issues.

Kwame Nkrumah: Kwame Nkrumah was a Ghanaian nationalist leader who led the country to independence from British colonial rule in 1957. He became the first Prime Minister and later the President of Ghana and was a leading advocate of Pan-Africanism.

Peter Mensah: Peter Mensah is a Ghanaian-British actor who has appeared in numerous films and television series, including "300", "Spartacus", and "Agents of S.H.I.E.L.D.". He has also been involved in various humanitarian and charitable causes, including the fight against Ebola in West Africa.

Abedi Pele: Abedi Pele is a retired Ghanaian footballer who is widely regarded as one of the greatest African footballers of all time. He won the African Footballer of the Year award three times and led the Ghanaian national team to its first-ever appearance in the FIFA World Cup in 2006.

Patrick Awuah: Patrick Awuah is a Ghanaian entrepreneur and educator who founded Ashesi University, a private liberal arts university in Ghana. He has been recognized for his efforts to promote education and entrepreneurship in Africa and was awarded the MacArthur Genius Grant in 2015.

Ofosu Yeboah: Emmanuel Ofosu Yeboah is a Ghanaian athlete and activist who has overcome physical disabilities to become an advocate for disability rights in Africa. He gained international attention when he cycled across Ghana on a single leg to raise awareness about the abilities of people with disabilities.

Esther Afua Ocloo: Esther Afua Ocloo was a Ghanaian entrepreneur and pioneer of microfinance in Africa. She founded Women's World Banking, a global microfinance organization that provides financial services to low-income women.

Rebecca Akufo-Addo: Rebecca Akufo-Addo is a Ghanaian philanthropist and the First Lady of Ghana. She has been actively involved in various charitable and humanitarian causes, including the fight against breast cancer and the promotion of early childhood education.

Reggie Rockstone: Reggie Rockstone is a Ghanaian rapper and music producer who is widely regarded as the "Godfather of Hiplife", a music genre that blends hip-hop with highlife music. He has been instrumental in popularizing hiplife music in Ghana and has collaborated with numerous international artists.

These Ghanaians have made significant contributions in various fields, and their impact has been felt beyond the borders of Ghana. They have shown that Ghanaians can succeed and make a difference in the world with hard work, determination, and talent.

7.7. GHANA'S VULNERABILITY TO CLIMATE CHANGE IMPACTS, INCLUDING SEA LEVEL RISE AND DROUGHT

Like many African countries, Ghana is vulnerable to climate change impacts, including sea level rise, drought, floods, and other extreme weather events. The country's economy is heavily reliant on agriculture, which is sensitive to changes in climate patterns. Climate change is, therefore, a significant threat to Ghana's development efforts and socio-economic progress.

Sea level rise is one of Ghana's most significant threats to coastal communities. The country's coastline stretches over 550 km, with many communities and urban centres near the coast. A significant rise in sea level due to climate change could lead to coastal erosion, flooding, and displacement of people living in these areas. The government of Ghana has been implementing measures to address this issue, including the construction of sea defence walls and other infrastructure.

Drought is another significant threat to Ghana's development. The country's northern regions are already prone to frequent droughts, and climate change is expected to exacerbate this problem. Droughts can lead to crop failures, food insecurity, and displacement of people. The government of Ghana has been implementing measures to mitigate the impacts of drought, including the construction of dams and other water storage infrastructure.

Floods are also a significant threat to Ghana's development. The country has experienced several floods in recent years, causing significant damage to infrastructure and displacing people. Climate change is expected to increase the frequency and intensity of floods in the country. The government of Ghana has been implementing measures to address this issue, including the construction of drainage systems and other flood control infrastructure.

In addition to these impacts, climate change also affects Ghana's natural resources, including its forests, fisheries, and wildlife. Deforestation, for instance, is a significant contributor to climate change and leads to the country's biodiversity loss. The government of Ghana has been implementing sustainable forest management practices and promoting alternative livelihoods for communities living near forests.

Overall, Ghana's vulnerability to climate change underscores the need for the country to take urgent and decisive action to address this issue. The Ghanaian government has implemented several policies and initiatives to address these challenges to promote sustainable land use, conservation, and the development of renewable energy sources. These include the National Climate Change Policy, the Forest and Wildlife Policy, the Renewable Energy Act, and the Green Ghana Project, which aims to plant five million trees nationwide to mitigate deforestation.

However, the success of these policies is hindered by several challenges, including limited resources, weak institutional capacity, and inadequate public awareness of climate change issues. To overcome these challenges, Ghana needs to strengthen its institutional capacity, improve its access to climate finance, and increase public awareness of climate change and its impacts.

In conclusion, climate change significantly impacts Ghana's economy and environment, and addressing these challenges requires a comprehensive and coordinated response from all stakeholders, including the government, private sector, and civil society. By promoting sustainable land use, conservation, and the development of renewable energy sources, Ghana can mitigate the impacts of climate change and build a more resilient and sustainable economy and environment.

7.8. THE POTENTIAL FOR GREEN GROWTH AND SUSTAINABLE DEVELOPMENT IN GHANA

Like many other developing countries, Ghana faces the dual challenge of economic growth and sustainable development. With increasing global concern about climate change, the need for green growth and sustainable development has become more important than ever. Fortunately, Ghana has a lot of potential for green growth, which, if harnessed, could help the country achieve its development goals while preserving the environment.

Renewable energy. Ghana has abundant renewable energy resources, such as solar, wind, and hydro, which, if harnessed, could help the country transition from its current reliance on fossil fuels to a more sustainable and environmentally friendly energy mix. The government has taken steps to promote renewable energy development, including the Renewable Energy Act and the establishment of the Renewable Energy Fund. Private sector investments in the renewable energy sector have also been growing in recent years.

Sustainable agriculture. Agriculture is a critical sector of Ghana's economy, providing livelihoods for a significant portion of the population. However, unsustainable agricultural practices such as slash-and-burn agriculture, overgrazing, and deforestation have led to soil erosion, land degradation, and biodiversity loss. The government has implemented policies to promote sustainable agriculture, including the Planting for Food and Jobs program, which aims to increase productivity while conserving the environment.

Sustainable tourism is also an area of potential for green growth. Ghana's rich cultural heritage and diverse natural attractions could attract more tourists. However, tourism can also have negative environmental impacts, such as the overuse of resources and pollution. The government has taken steps to promote sustainable tourism, including developing ecotourism sites and promoting community-based tourism.

Waste management is another area of potential for green growth. Ghana faces a significant waste management challenge, with most waste ending up in landfills or littering the streets. However, waste can also be a valuable resource, and if managed properly, it could generate income and reduce environmental pollution. The government has implemented policies to promote waste segregation and recycling, and private sector investments in the waste management sector have been growing in recent years.

Overall, Ghana has significant potential for green growth and sustainable development. While there are still many challenges to overcome, the government's commitment to promoting sustainable development and reducing the negative impacts of economic growth provides a strong foundation for future progress.

In conclusion, Ghana has a lot of potential for green growth and sustainable development. The government has implemented policies to promote renewable energy, sustainable agriculture, sustainable tourism, and waste management. Private sector investments in these sectors have also been growing. These potential areas could help Ghana achieve its development goals while preserving the environment if harnessed.

8. Infrastructure in Ghana

8.1. POWER IN GHANA

Ghana has a population of over 30 million. Of this, around 86% had access to electricity in 2020, a share gradually reached over the previous years. For instance, as of 2010, only about 64% of the population could access electricity. The prevalence of access is usually higher in urban areas than in rural communities. Moreover, the country's total number of individuals without electricity increased to around 4.4 million in 2020. Despite the annually increasing electricity supply nationwide, frequent power outages have remained problematic. These have often been attributed to electricity transmission challenges faced by the energy institutions in the country.

Ghana has a vibrant power generation sector, with public and private companies involved in it. Reforms in the power sector in the 1980s gradually removed barriers. They created a level playing field for the participation of independent power producers in an area that public sector participants had previously dominated.

Hydro and thermal generation fueled by crude oil, natural gas, and diesel remain Ghana's power supply sources. Ghana also exports power to Togo, Benin, and Burkina Faso. Ongoing grid expansions, which include the completion of transmission lines and Bulk Supply Points (BSPs) across the nation, will allow further exports to other neighbouring countries in the sub-region.

The total installed capacity for existing plants in Ghana is 5,134 Megawatt (MW), with a dependable capacity of 4,710 MW. Thermal generation accounts for the largest share of Ghana's power generation, representing 66% , with hydro accounting for 33% .

The growing energy demand and customer base often outweigh the electricity supply in the country. 2021, for instance, electricity demand was expected to reach around 21.3 thousand gigawatt hours. Contrary to this high demand, generating companies sent out approximately 18 thousand gigawatt hours of electricity to distribution companies, mines, and for exports in 2020.

8.2. EDUCATION AND TRAINING

Ghana has 17,212 students studying abroad, according to UNESCO, and 56.08% of the population in Ghana is under 25 years of age.

The Education System: Ghana has pioneered modern mass education in West Africa. First introduced in Christian missionary schools and colonial government schools, most notably in coastal areas during formal British rule after 1867, Ghana's government greatly expanded modern European-style education after achieving independence in 1957. The introduction of free and compulsory basic education in 1961 was a veritable milestone achievement that greatly helped advance access to education, as was the founding of the first Ghanaian universities: the University of Ghana, established initially under British rule in 1948, and the Kwame Nkrumah University of Science and Technology (KNUST), opened in 1952.

Adinkra is a set of symbols developed by the Akan, used to represent concepts and aphorisms. Saturated with meaning, these symbols have come to symbolize the richness of Akan culture and serve as a shorthand for communicating deep truths in visual form long before the European education. As an example, the fact that most universities in Ghana use at least one Adinkra symbol in their logo demonstrates the gravitas their use has come to symbolize.

Adinkra Symbols

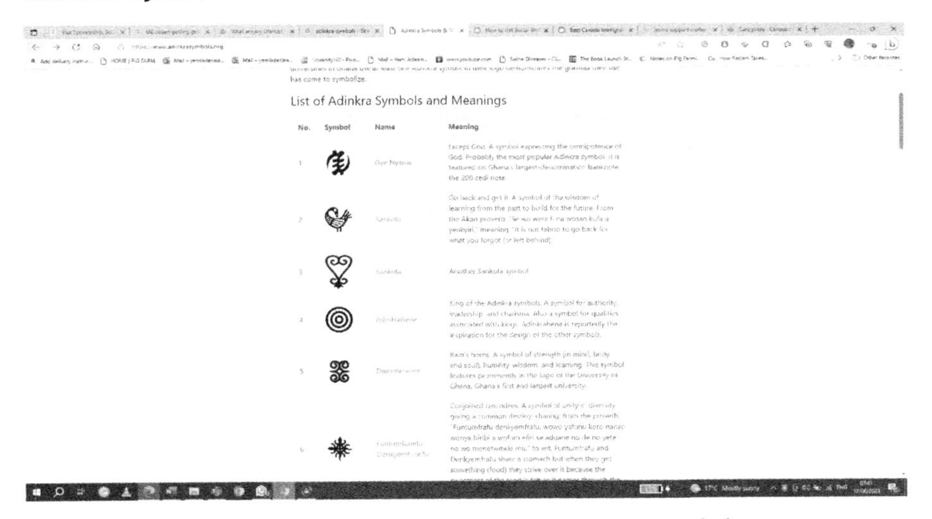

has come to symbolize.

List of Adinkra Symbols and Meanings

No.	Symbol	Name	Meaning
1		Gye Nyame	Except God. A symbol expressing the omnipotence of God. Probably the most popular Adinkra symbol. It is featured on Ghana's largest-denomination banknote, the 200 cedi note.
2		Sankofa	Go back and get it. A symbol of the wisdom of learning from the past to build for the future. From the Akan proverb, "Se wo were fi na wosan kofa a yenkyiri," meaning "It is not taboo to go back for what you forgot (or left behind)."
3		Sankofa	Another Sankofa symbol
4		Adinkrahene	King of the Adinkra symbols. A symbol for authority, leadership, and charisma. Also a symbol for qualities associated with kings. Adinkrahene is reportedly the inspiration for the design of the other symbols.
5		[illegible]	Ram's horns. A symbol of strength (in mind, body and soul), humility, wisdom, and learning. This symbol features prominently in the logo of the University of Ghana, Ghana's first and largest university.
6		Funtunfunefu Denkyemfunefu	Conjoined crocodiles. A symbol of unity in diversity giving a common destiny sharing; from the proverb "Funtumfrafu denkyemfrafu, wowo yafunu koro nanso wonya biribi a wofom efiri se aduane no de no yete no wo menetwitwie mu," to wit, Funtumfrafu and Denkyemfrafu share a stomach but when they get something (food) they strive over it because the

Adinkra Symbols and Meanings. Source: *adinkrasymbols.com*

Elementary education in Ghana begins at six and is nominally free of charge at public schools. However, even public schools charge fees for various items like teaching materials or uniforms, so education is not entirely free.

The elementary school curriculum focuses on developing basic reading and writing abilities, arithmetic, and problem-solving skills. The subjects taught include English, local languages in early grades, mathematics, social studies, integrated science, arts, physical education, and civics. Elementary education concludes with the completion of grade six.

The West African Examinations Council (WAEC): After independence, British West African countries successfully transitioned from using a U.K.-based school curriculum to the examination format of the regional WAEC. Originally established in the 1950s as a means to "harmonize and standardize pre-university assessment procedures in British West Africa", the Council is now an international organization with five member states: Ghana, Nigeria, Sierra Leone, the Gambia, as well as Liberia, the only non-British colony to join the council (in 1974).

Ghana's government has taken several initiatives to improve the social conditions of its citizens. As a result, the country has witnessed a significant improvement in the quality of life of its citizens. Education is one of the most important factors that contribute to social development. Ghana's government has made significant investments in education over the years. The country has made primary education free and compulsory for all children, and the government has also increased its spending on education. As a result, Ghana has achieved a literacy rate of over 70%, significantly higher than the average for sub-Saharan Africa. The government has also made efforts to improve access to higher education by increasing the number of universities in the country

8.3. HEALTH

The Government of Ghana continues to expand access to healthcare coverage and the scope of benefits it makes available to its citizens. Ghana's 2021 census results report 68.6 % of the population is covered by either the National Health

Insurance Scheme (NHIS) or private health insurance plans. There is a higher rate of health insurance coverage for females (72.6%) than males (64.5%). Health insurance coverage ranges from a low of 51.9% in the Oti Region to a high of 86.2 % in the Upper East Region. Ghana has moved away from a 'pay as you go' system, where individual health expenditures were paid in cash before treatment and covered entirely by patients. The National Health Insurance Scheme now provides wide coverage for a limited scope of health issues, primarily insuring for treatment against the most prevalent diseases, such as malaria.

The healthcare sector in Ghana is organized at three different levels: national, regional, and district. Health interventions are defined for each level and are delivered at the respective clinics and hospitals.

Healthcare is variable throughout Ghana. Urban centres are well-served and are where most hospitals, clinics, and pharmacies in the country can be found. Rural areas often have no modern healthcare services, and patients in these areas either rely on traditional African medicine or travel great distances for healthcare. The government provides most healthcare, and it is primarily administered by the Ministry of Health and the Ghana Health Services.

Ghana spends, on average, about 6% of its GDP on healthcare infrastructure. Ghana has very limited local pharmaceutical production and even less medical equipment and device manufacturing, and the country relies on imports for approximately 85% of its total healthcare consumption.

As a result, Ghana has witnessed a decline in infant mortality rates, and life expectancy has increased. The government has also tried combatting diseases like malaria and HIV/AIDS.

Poverty reduction and gender equality are important factors contributing to social development. Ghana has made significant progress in reducing poverty over the years, with poverty rates declining from over 50% in the 1990s to around 23% in 2016. The government has also made efforts to promote gender equality, and women's representation in government has increased. However, there is still a long way to go, and Ghana's government needs to continue improving social conditions in the country.

8.4. GHANA'S FUTURE IN THE GLOBAL ARENA

Ghana, located in West Africa, has experienced significant economic and political growth in the past few decades. Its economy has been growing steadily, and it has become a hub for foreign investment, particularly in the areas of oil and gas. Ghana is also recognized for its democracy and political stability. As Ghana continues to develop and expand its presence in the global arena, it is essential to consider its future prospects.

One aspect of Ghana's future in the global arena is its potential to become a leader in African trade. Ghana has been actively pursuing trade partnerships with other African nations, and it has also been working to increase its exports of non-traditional goods, such as processed foods and textiles. By focusing on these areas, Ghana can help to drive economic growth across the continent and strengthen its position as a key player in the African economy.

Another important consideration for Ghana's future is its ability to attract foreign investment. While the country has already seen significant investment in its oil and gas industries, there are other sectors where Ghana has the potential to excel, such as agriculture and technology. By creating a business-friendly environment and investing in infrastructure and education, Ghana can continue to attract foreign investors and position itself as a leader in these industries. Ghana has been actively pursuing trade partnerships with other African nations, such as through the African Continental Free Trade Area (AfCFTA), which aims to create a single market for goods and services across the continent. For example, the Ghanaian company Kasapreko Limited has been exporting its locally-made alcoholic beverages to other African countries, such as Nigeria and South Africa, under the AfCFTA.

In addition to its oil and gas industries, Ghana has the potential to excel in other sectors, such as agriculture and technology. For example, Ghana's cocoa industry is one of the largest in the world, and the country is also the second-largest producer of gold in Africa. Furthermore, Ghana has been investing in technology and innovation by creating the Ghana Innovation Hub, which aims to support startups and entrepreneurs in the tech sector.

Ghana has also been addressing social and environmental challenges as part of its development efforts. For example, the government launched the National Social Protection Policy in 2016 to provide a safety net for vulnerable populations such as children, the elderly, and persons with disabilities. Additionally, Ghana has been promoting renewable energy sources such as solar power and has set a target of 10% of its energy mix being from renewable sources by 2020. These efforts demonstrate Ghana's commitment to sustainable and inclusive development.

Finally, Ghana's future in the global arena will depend on its ability to address social and environmental challenges. Poverty, inequality, and environmental degradation are all issues that could hinder Ghana's development and its ability to compete on the world stage. By prioritizing policies and initiatives that address these challenges, Ghana can ensure that its growth is sustainable and inclusive and continues to impact the global community positively.

9. Conclusion

In this book, we have examined the question of whether the world needs Ghana. We have explored Ghana's history, culture, economy, and politics and analysed the country's contributions to the world and the challenges and opportunities it faces. In this final chapter, we summarize the key arguments and findings of the book and emphasize the importance of supporting Ghana's development efforts.

Ghana has played a significant role in shaping the history and culture of Africa and the world. It was the first country in Africa to gain independence from colonial rule and has been a leader in the fight for African liberation and self-determination. Ghana has also contributed significantly to the arts, music, and literature and has led regional and global political and economic organizations.

Despite these achievements, Ghana faces significant challenges in its development efforts. These include the impact of slavery and colonialism on its development trajectory, the challenge of managing its natural resources sustainably, and the impact of corruption and political instability on its progress. However, Ghana has made significant efforts to overcome these challenges and has implemented initiatives to promote economic growth, reduce poverty, and improve governance.

Ghana's potential to become a leading player in the global economy is significant. The country's strategic location, natural resources, and political stability make it an attractive destination for investment and trade. Ghana has also shown a commitment to building a sustainable future through initiatives to promote renewable energy, environmental conservation, and the achievement of the Sustainable Developmental Goals.

The international community must continue to support Ghana's development efforts. This support can take the form of investment in key sectors such as agriculture, infrastructure, and education and through partnerships and collaborations with Ghanaian organizations and institutions. It is also important that the international community recognizes and values Ghana's contributions to the world and continues to engage with the country on issues of regional and global importance.

In conclusion, Ghana has a significant role to play in shaping the future of Africa and the world. The country's rich history, vibrant culture, and strategic location make it an important player in regional and global affairs. By supporting Ghana's development efforts, we can help to ensure that this potential is realized, and that Ghana continues to make positive contributions to the world.

10. Glossary

Here is a glossary of some terms and concepts that may be useful for readers of this book:

Aid Dependency: The situation where a country becomes overly reliant on foreign aid as a source of income, often leading to a lack of self-sufficiency and sustainable economic growth.

Brain Drain: The migration of highly skilled and educated individuals from developing countries to developed countries, often resulting in a loss of talent and expertise in the country of origin.

Decolonization: The process of gaining independence from a colonial power and establishing self-rule in a formerly colonized country.

Diaspora: A community of people who share a common ethnic or cultural identity and live outside their country of origin.

Foreign Direct Investment (FDI): Investment by a foreign company or individual in a business or industry in another country, often to generate profits or gain access to new markets.

Human Development Index (HDI): A country's development measure based on life expectancy, education, and income per capita.

Microfinance: Financial services, such as small loans and savings accounts, provided to low-incomes

Neocolonialism: The use of economic and political power by developed countries to control the policies and economies of developing countries.

Pan-Africanism: A movement advocating for the unity and solidarity of African people across the continent and in the diaspora.

Sustainable Development: Development that meets the needs of the present without compromising the ability of future generations to meet their own needs while also considering economic, social, and environmental factors.

Structural Adjustment Programs (SAPs): Economic policies imposed on developing countries by international financial institutions as a condition for receiving loans or debt relief. These policies often involve austerity measures, privatization, and trade liberalization.

Technology Transfer: The process of sharing technology, knowledge, and expertise between countries, often from developed to developing countries, to facilitate economic growth and development.

Universal Basic Education: A system of education that provides free and compulsory primary education to all children, aiming to promote greater educational attainment and reduce inequalities in access to education.

World System Theory: A theory that explains global economic and political relations as a hierarchical system where developed countries dominate and exploit developing countries for their own benefit.

11. References

Here are some references that may be useful for readers interested in further exploring the topics covered in this book:

Akyeampong, E. (2006). Africa's Economic Development: Beyond the Dependency Paradigm. Harvard University Press.

Aryeetey, E., Nissanke, M., & Weder, B. (2014). Institutional Change and Economic Development in Ghana. Oxford University Press.

Ayittey, G. B. N. (2011). Africa Betrayed. Palgrave Macmillan.

Appiah, K. A. (2010). The Honor Code: How Moral Revolutions Happen. W. W. Norton & Company.

Beyond income, beyond averages, beyond today: Inequalities in human development in the 21st century. United Nations Development Programme.

Chazan, N. (2018). Politics and Society in Contemporary Africa. Palgrave Macmillan.

Collins, R. O. (2008). Ghana's Political Transition 1990-2000: The Impact of International Aid and Christopher Ehret, The Civilizations of Africa, (Charlottesville: University of Virginia Press, 2002)

External Influence. Ashgate Publishing, Ltd.

Debrah, Y. A., & Agyei-Mensah, S. (Eds.). (2013). Labor and Development in Ghana. Routledge.

David Conrad, Empires of Medieval West Africa: Ghana, Mali, Songhay, (New York: Facts on File, 2005)

David Christian, Cynthia Brown, Craig Benjamin, Big History: Between nothing and everything, (New York: McGraw, 2014)

Dierk Lange, Ancient Kingdoms of West Africa, (Dettlebach: Verlag J.H. Roll, 2004)

Gyasi, K. O., & Arko-Adjei, A. (2015). Corruption and Human Development in Africa: The Case of Ghana. Palgrave Macmillan.

Goldstein, A., & Udry, C. (2008). The Profits of Power: Land Rights and Agricultural Investment in Ghana. Journal of Political Economy, 116(6), 981-1022.

Institute of Statistical, Social and Economic Research (ISSER). (2017). Ghana in Transition: Perspectives on Economic and Social Development. University of Ghana.

Kwakye, M. O. (2017). The Ghana Reader: History, Culture, Politics. Duke University Press.

Nehemia Levtzion, Ancient Ghana and Mali, (London: Methuen, 1973)

Nehemia Levtzion and Jay Spaulding, Medieval West Africa: Views from Arab scholars and merchants, (Princeton: Markus Wiener, 2003)

Patrick Munson, "Archaeology and the prehistoric origins of the Ghana Em-pire" Journal of African Studies (1980) vol. 21, no. 4

Nugent, P. (2013). Africa Since Independence: A Comparative History. Palgrave Macmillan.

Owusu, F. Y., & Oduro, A. D. (2018). Bridging the Development Divide in Ghana: Strategic Partnership Opportunities. Springer.

Owusu, M. (2015). Ghana Beyond Aid: A Critical Discourse. Ghana University Press.

Robert Cohen, Discovering the Empire of Ghana, (New York: Rosen Publishing, 2013)UNESCO. (2017). Culture and Sustainable Development in the Pacific. UNESCO.

United Nations Development Programme (UNDP). (2019). Human Development Report 2019: United Nations. (2015). Transforming our world: the 2030 Agenda for Sustainable Development. United Nations.

World Bank. (2020). Ghana Economic Outlook. World Bank.

World Health Organization (WHO). (2017). Ghana Country Health Profile. WHO.

Yeboah, I., & Owusu, G. (2016). Environmental and Resource Economics in Ghana. Springer.

https://theculturetrip.com/africa/ghana/articles/12-traditions-and-customs-only-ghanaians-can-understand/

https://blog.compassion.com/traditions-of-ghana-warrior-king/

https://www.commisceo-global.com/resources/country-guides/ghana-guide

https://www.britannica.com/place/Ghana/Daily-life-and-social-customs

https://www.afsusa.org/countries/ghana/

https://www.worldatlas.com/articles/the-culture-of-ghana.html

https://www.cultureready.org/blog/ghanaian-customs-help-you-understand-culture

https://www.everyculture.com/Ge-It/Ghana.html